TO

TORRES

ANFIELD SIGNINGS: THE HITS, MISSES AND RECORD BREAKERS

Sport Media
A Trinity Mirror Business

WRITTEN BY: Paul Hassall **PRODUCED BY:** Roy Gilfoyle & Jamie Dunmore
EXECUTIVE EDITOR: Ken Rogers **EDITOR:** Steve Hanrahan **ART EDITOR:** Rick Cooke **PRODUCTION EDITOR:** Paul Dove

WRITERS: David Randles, Chris McLoughlin, Gavin Kirk, John Hynes
DESIGN TEAM: Lee Ashun, Barry Parker, Colin Sumpter, Glen Hind, Alison Gilliland, James Kenyon
PHOTOGRAPHY: Trinity Mirror, Empics **PRINTERS:** Pensord
SALES & MARKETING MANAGER: Elizabeth Morgan 0151 285 8412
Write to: Sport Media, PO BOX 48, Liverpool, L69 3EB

FROM TOSHACK TO TORRES...

There is a unique buzz and feel good factor associated with the sight of Liverpool's latest signing being paraded in front of the watching world whilst sporting both a wide grin and the famous red shirt.

It is the highlight of the summer and a time when the fans' topic of conversation switches from analysis of our last match to speculating over the players we should sign in order to bring our long wait for the Premiership title to an end.

But this year's transfer window has been slightly different.

It has been one of the most anticipated in recent memory and one that has been heralded as a new dawn under the club's American owners George Gillett and Tom Hicks.

Last season may well have ended in despair following the disappointing defeat to AC Milan in Athens but with a manager who has led us to two Champions League finals in just three years finally being given the funds to compete with Chelsea and Manchester United, a huge wave of expectation and optimism has been sweeping across Merseyside.

The arrival of several exciting players, including the club record £20million signing of Fernando Torres, has shown the club's intent to keep strides with the big spenders and re-establish itself at the summit of English football.

But splashing the cash does not always guarantee success and there have been times throughout our post-war history that have seen us both celebrate and bemoan our latest new recruit.

From Shankly to Benitez we have experienced the full spectrum of top signings through to the ones that did not work out.

In this souvenir special we take a walk down memory lane and identify some of the best and worst new recruits over the years while we also take a look at our record signings, the cult heroes who may or may not have made the grade and the new boys of 2007.

With the Premiership season just under two weeks away the anticipation among Red fans across the world is reaching fever point as Rafa concludes what could go down as one of the most important summer spending sprees in the club's history.

Can Fernando Torres prove to be as good for Liverpool as fellow record signing John Toshack?

The stars are bright

9 fernando

30 YEARS ON FROM DALGLISH REPLACING KEEGAN . . . WILL TORRES BE THE NEW FOWLER?

IN 1977 Liverpool broke their transfer record to sign a striker that would go on to attain the status of the greatest player in the club's history.

His name was Kenny Dalglish and although fans were still mourning the departure of Kevin Keegan when he arrived, he took over the famous number seven shirt and would eventually surpass his predecessor's achievements and establish himself as the undisputed King of the Kop.

30 years on and we could be seeing a similar story unfolding.

A Reds legend by the name of Robbie Fowler has departed, leaving both the number nine shirt and a huge void in the hearts of all kopites.

For his replacement we have broken the club transfer record to sign a player touted as one of the best young strikers in Europe.

He is a man known as 'El Nino' (The Kid) or El Nino de Oro (The Golden Boy) and for the past six years he has lit up La Liga with a repertoire of sublime strikes.

He made his first-team debut at the age of 17, was captain by 19 and has long since been thought of as the most promising youngster in Spain.

Like Fowler, Fernando José Torres Sanz was revered and idolised by the fans of his hometown club and he has already made the right impression with the Reds faithful after he was seen sporting the inscription 'We'll never walk alone' on the inside of his Atletico Madrid skipper's armband last season.

It was merely a present from his closest circle of friends but gave the watching world a huge hint as to what his preferred destination would be if he were to leave his spiritual home.

For years he has been one of the most sought after players in Europe but when Liverpool finally came calling, hoping to make him the first big money signing under Tom Hicks and George Gillett, he insisted they were the only club he was interested in.

On completing his £20million transfer to Anfield last month he revealed his excitement at the prospect of spearheading Liverpool's quest for Premiership glory.

"As soon as I heard of Liverpool's interest I said to Atletico 'please will you allow me to speak to them?' I told them

F. TORRES
9
adidas

‘IT IS A BIG LEAP FOR ME AND I THINK IT WAS THE RIGHT DECISION FOR EVERYONE’

that this is the offer they must take seriously and they did," he told LFC magazine in an exclusive interview.

"I didn't pay attention or listen to any other offers once I knew Liverpool were interested.

"It is a big leap for me and I think it was the right decision for everyone.

"Yes it was difficult to leave Atletico, the club I have supported all my life but I have always been aware of and followed Liverpool's great history. To have a chance of playing a part in that is too good an opportunity to turn down."

Such a desire to play for the Reds is exactly what fans expect of new recruits and having grown up in a similar working class environment with Atletico he is in no doubt as to how important the followers in the stand are.

"The fans are very important to me," he said.

"I was always a fan of Atletico before I was fortunate enough to play for them so I have seen it from both sides. That used to be me on the other side of the barrier waiting for autographs so I know what it's like.

"I am very aware that the fans here at Liverpool are also very important. The fact that they get behind you whether you are winning, losing or drawing is very, very special and doesn't happen everywhere.

"As a player you need to pay that support back."

One man who is confident Torres will do this is Reds boss Rafael Benitez.

The Spaniard is convinced his compatriot can recapture the form that made him such a star in Madrid and feels our new number nine has all the attributes to make a crucial impact.

"When you talk about top strikers there aren't too many around with the quality Fernando has," said Rafa.

"We are happy to have him here. At just 23 he is one of the best young

TORRES FACTFILE

Full name
Fernando José Torres Sanz

Date of birth
March 20, 1984 (age 23)

Place of birth
Madrid, Spain

Height
1.86m (6ft 1in)

Position
Striker

Former Club
Atletico Madrid (2001-07)
Appearances 214 Goals 82

National team
Spain (2003–)
Appearances 40 Goals 14

forwards in Spain and a lot of people were talking about him. His commitment to Atletico was fantastic and I think he deserved to be captain.

"He was the icon of the team and always played with the passion that supporters wanted to see.

"I am sure he will be a good player for the supporters. It won't take long for them to see that he can fight and work hard and give everything in every game."

Rafa acknowledges that a lot will rest on Torres' shoulders after the club smashed their transfer record to prise him away from Atletico but he also believes that in today's market, Torres will prove to be an astute piece of business for the Reds.

"We needed to decide on all the right details if we were to pay big money for a player like this," he said.

"It is good business for both in terms of the player on the pitch and also in terms of his age. He is only 23 but has been playing at a good level since the age of 17 so has experience too.

"If you look at the potential he has, that can only benefit us in the future."

EL FICHAJE DE 'EL NIÑO' POR EL LIVERPOOL ESTÁ MÁS CERCA QUE NUNCA

TORRES, COLORÍN COLORADO

'HE HAS ALL THE ATTRIBUTES TO BECOME FIRMLY ESTABLISHED AS WORLD CLASS'

REACTION TO THE SIGNING OF FERNANDO TORRES . . .

"Torres has all the attributes to become firmly established as world class. Some of the other players we're being linked with excite me too. It's great to see us looking at young, hungry players with their best years ahead of them."

"Not only is he a great player now, potentially he has all the attributes to become firmly established as world class. He's at the right club and will be working with the right people to make that happen.

"He's a fast, strong centre forward who likes the ball being played into his feet. They are the kind of strikers I love playing with. I've no doubt we're going to get our money's worth out of him, with him being such a young player."

STEVEN GERRARD

"I think he'll be a great player for Liverpool. To be honest I'm a Liverpool fan and I hope he brings the championship to Liverpool.

"Since I've been playing, we've never won that, and as I said before I'm a fan, so I want Liverpool to win everything.

"Players signing of this calibre will only help the club to get in a position where they can challenge for titles."

ROBBIE FOWLER

"I think to compete for the league you're looking for someone to get maybe 20-25 goals a season and Torres looks to be that.

"He's got the ability and capability to do it.

"He can kick with both feet, which I think is always a great asset for a striker.

"Liverpool don't need players to come in and learn the ropes, they need players to come straight into the side and Torres fits that. "

IAN RUSH

"He (Torres) has already demonstrated his enormous quality and to have him in the team would be brilliant."

XABI ALONSO

"You have a great pedigree there. He is a young lad, very quick, which is good for the Premiership and hopefully he will do very well."

JAMIE CARRAGHER

"We need a player that scores 20 or 25 goals a season and Fernando Torres can be that man.

"He has many virtues. I am confident that he will do very important things for the team. It's true that the style of football is different in England. But we want him to be ready from the first minute and show the player he has been in recent years."

PEPE REINA

"Liverpool have done a very good job in getting him because Torres is such a good player.

"I'm surprised Atletico have sold their captain. Since he started to play for them he has been a regular player and important to the team.

"England is a good place for his qualities. He has a strong personality, but he's also quick and strong physically.

"He's also a very skilful player especially in one-on-one situations, which will be something different for Liverpool up front. They have not had a striker who can take the ball and beat opponents."

RADOMIR ANTIC, former Atletico boss.

THIS IS
LIVERPOOL
FOOTBALL CLUB
ANFIELD
adidas
Carlsberg

'I AM SO EXCITED ABOUT SEEING HIM PLAY IN FRONT OF THE KIND OF ATMOSPHERE ANFIELD GENERATES'

GUILLEM BALAGUE WITH THE WORD FROM SPAIN . . .

"HE is only 23 now and is still a work in progress. He's not the finished product but he is still an outstanding player.

"I would put him on the same level as Wayne Rooney and the stats bear out that comparison.

"Atletico Madrid has always been a club which relies on counter attacking football and that has been, in a way, his success and his downfall.

"Obviously he fits very well into that system because of his explosive pace and his strength, and as a result he did very well very quickly for Atletico.

"But the problem is that you can get stuck in that type of role, as Michael Owen found out.

"Fernando is much more than just a counter attacking player.

"He is a very clever player, especially outside the penalty box, and I can see him forming very effective partnerships, especially with Dirk Kuyt.

"Fernando is prepared to do the dirty work outside the box, Kuyt is more effective inside, both are hard working, both are mobile and both can drift wide to complement the other."

Torres has agreed a six year contract at Liverpool, and Balague has warned that fans may have to be patient if they are to see the very best out of Torres.

But he believes it will be well worth the wait.

"Of course he will need time to adapt," he added. "People will have to be patient.

"He has always played up front on his own in Spain. Now he will have to play a different system and in a different league.

"It might not even be his first season before we see his best. Like Didier Drogba at Chelsea, we may have to wait until the second season before he can make his biggest impact.

"But he is very clever, on and off the pitch, and he is very humble.

"People may have to be patient while he adapts to English football but I am so excited about seeing him play in front of the kind of atmosphere Anfield generates.

"The fans there will love him.

"I have spoken to Steven Gerrard and Jamie Carragher and they are both very excited and I am very excited.

"He comes from a working class family from a working class district of Madrid and he became a working class hero," he said.

"The fans of Liverpool can relate to him and he can be a big success."

The day I signed . . .

"We had to get to Lytham St Anne's to complete the signing so I could play straight away. It's only about 10 minutes from Bloomfield Road, but Shanks was the worst driver in the world. Just as we left the ground he half went through a set of lights and a woman shunted into the back of us. A police car flags us down and the young officer comes up to the car. 'What is it officer?' Shanks asked. 'I'm sorry sir you can't continue in that car as you've got no lights'. said the policeman. 'Do you know who's in this car?', said Shanks. 'No' said the officer, 'I don't recognise you.' 'No not me you fool', he said, 'I've got the future captain of England alongside me.'"

EMLYN HUGHES

adidas
9

SUMMER OF SPENDING ON AMERICAN EXPRESS

LIVERPOOL'S CLOSE SEASON MOVES IN THE TRANSFER MARKET HAVE GOT ANFIELD FANS BUZZING. SO WHAT CAN WE EXPECT FROM THE REST OF RAFA'S MAIN ACQUISITIONS?

THE pursuit and capture of Spain international striker Fernando Torres has grabbed the majority of the headlines in what has been a busy summer of transfer activity at Anfield.

The £20million record deal has already caught the imagination of the fans in the city with the sighting of more than the odd red shirt sporting the name Torres with the number nine on the back.

But although the talented Spaniard has got all reds hoping he can be the latest in our long tradition of great strikers, he is not the only player to have been welcomed to Melwood.

The likes of Lucas Leiva, Yossi Benayoun and Ryan Babel are just a few of the new boys hoping to make an impact on the first-team next season and maybe even upstage the great El Nino.

Here we profile some of the other newcomers who have arrived courtesy of American Express...

RYAN BABEL

'MY MANAGER CALLED ME UP TO SAY THAT LIVERPOOL WERE INTERESTED IN ME. THAT WAS A VERY BIG SHOCK'

DURING his playing career Marco Van Basten was undoubtedly one of the finest strikers the game has ever seen.

He was an artist on the field of play, a lethal hitman blessed with an unerring ability to score goals.

He is one of the most respected figures in the game and so when the legendary Dutchman gives his opinion on who he rates as one of the hottest prospects in Europe it is worth taking notice.

The former AC Milan striker, who is now the current coach of the Dutch national side, knows a thing or two about what it means to be one of the world's top players and so when he went on record to liken Dutch starlet Ryan Babel to the legendary genius that is Thierry Henry it was a comparison that caused a stir among some of the continent's finest clubs.

But it is easy to see why Van Basten speaks so glowingly about the youngster.

His exhilarating pace and ability to beat opponents have been a feature of Ajax's play in recent years and yet despite all the hype surrounding his talent it is also important to recognise that while he could well become a 'masterpiece,' at the moment he is very much a 'work in progress.'

He still has a lot to prove having fired just 14 goals in 73 matches for the Amsterdam outfit and he has still to settle into a regular position, operating as both a winger and as a central striker.

However, his talent is there for all to see and when you consider he has already featured 14 times for his national side at the age of just 20, it is obvious that he has the potential to be one of the most exciting players on the planet.

A product of the famous Ajax youth

KNVB
9

BABEL steps up to the penalty spot for The Netherlands in the U-21 European Championships

system he has risen to prominence with a series of stunning displays for both the Amsterdam side and the Holland under-20 team, a run of form that has convinced Rafael Benitez to make him the third most expensive signing in the history of Liverpool Football Club.

Indeed, his lightning pace, silky skill and ability to lead the attack or raid from the flanks should add an extra dimension to the Reds' forward line and provide kopites with more than the odd moment of excitement over the coming years.

The youngster's starring role in the recent under-20 European championships, where he helped Holland retain the title, further enhanced his reputation and ultimately earned him a dream move to Anfield.

Reds boss Rafael Benitez had been watching the youngster with great interest and was delighted to secure his signature on a five-year contract.

"I'm really pleased to have signed Ryan because he is a player of great potential," said Benitez.

"There were a lot of big clubs interested in him. He is a very good player now, and in the future he

RYAN BABEL and YOSSI BENAYOUN meet their new manager at Anfield

could be fantastic."

Babel, who cut short his summer holiday in order to join the Reds, could not hide his delight at signing for one of Europe's leading clubs.

"The chance to sign for Liverpool is one that you just have to take," he said.

"It was all it a bit shocking for me at first.

"I was lying on a beach on my holidays after the Under-21's and my manager called me up to say that Liverpool were interested in me. That was a very big shock.

"But when an option like this one comes along, at Liverpool with Rafael Benitez, then you don't think about it too long. You take it and that's what I did, without hesitation. No second thoughts."

Babel admits that the mere thought of playing in the famous red shirt was more than enough to convince him to leave Holland, but after speaking with Benitez it completely sold him on the transfer and now he cannot wait to get his Liverpool career under way.

"Rafa was very good with me," he said.

"It was important to me not just to be moving somewhere where I wouldn't play often. I wanted the right move and I think I have it. He has a lot of clear ideas about how he wants his football to be played and a lot of knowledge about the sport. He is going to be good for my education; he will help me to learn."

With the likes of Fernando Torres, Dirk Kuyt, Peter Crouch and Andriy Voronin already vying for a starting place in the Liverpool side, Babel acknowledges that he will have to produce his best form to retain a position in the team.

But while he admits his preferred position is as part of a front two, he is more than happy, and capable enough, to operate on both the left and right flanks.

"I would say that my best position is up front as part of a two-man attack either right up front or as the second striker," he revealed.

"That was where I played at the European Under-21 championships.

"But I can also play very happily on the right and the left of the pitch too, and the manager here agrees. He said to me that he thinks I can play in four positions for him and that's good to hear.

"He took a lot of time to explain his thoughts to me and that was special."

YOSSI BENAYOUN

'WHEN A CLUB LIKE LIVERPOOL SHOWS AN INTEREST IN YOU THEN YOU CANNOT REFUSE THEM'

AN Israeli international known for his flair and invention, Yossi Benayoun is hoping to prove his doubters wrong following his transfer from Premiership rivals West Ham United.

The midfield man made no secret of his desire to make the switch to Anfield and he finally landed his dream move when Rafa Benitez reportedly parted with £4million to secure his services.

While the Reds have been linked with a host of Europe's top wingers it is the former Racing Santander midfielder who caught Benitez's eye with a series of scintillating displays for the Hammers.

Some fans may have their doubts about the 27-year-old but Rafa is convinced he can fill the void left by the departure of Luis Garcia.

"Luis is a player who scores more goals and Benayoun tends to make more assists," said Rafa, after he was asked about the similarities between his new signing and Garcia.

"Like Luis, he is a very technical, clever player with a lot of game intelligence. He can also play in many positions, giving us a different option for the team.

"I first saw him play for Racing Santander in La Liga when he was a really good player, but when he first came to England we were watching to be sure he could adapt to a different style of football.

"It's clear he's done this very well at West Ham. Liverpool fans will remember how he played in the FA Cup Final against us when he was outstanding. We thought then this was a player who is capable of stepping up to a higher level."

Benayoun, who will become the club's new number 11, is in no doubts as to the magnitude of his move and while he still holds a fondness for West Ham, he can't wait to make his mark with Liverpool.

"I am very excited to be at a big club like Liverpool and it is a dream for me," said the Israel captain.

"I had a good time at West Ham but when a club like Liverpool shows an interest in you then you cannot refuse them.

"This is the biggest move of my career and I am at a club that fights for trophies every season.

"I'm 27 now and I am ready for this challenge. I know the Premiership. I want to work hard in every game and every training session in order to produce my best."

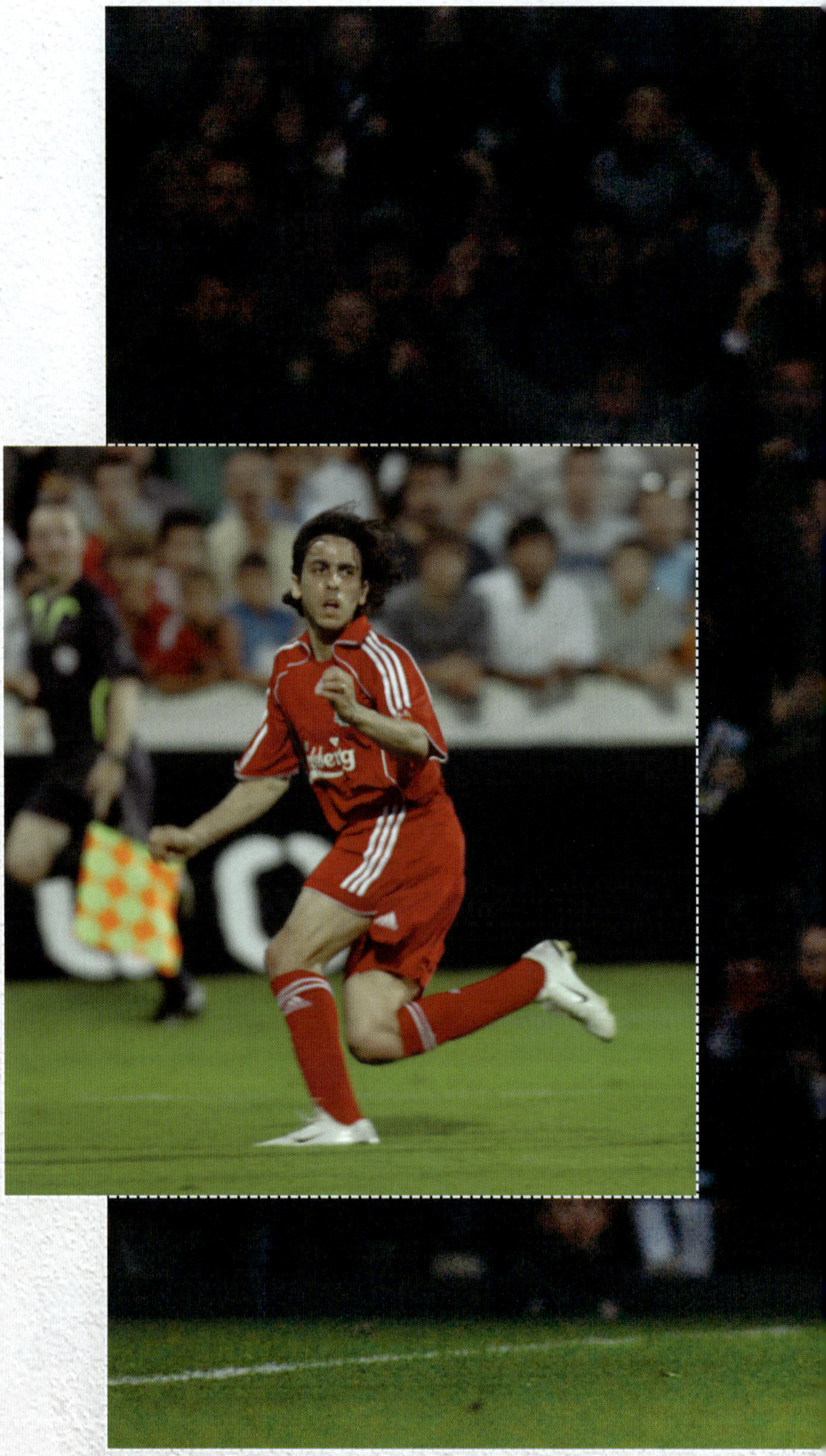

jobserve
15

ANDRIY VORONIN

'WE'VE GOT A LOT TO LOOK FORWARD TO AND I WANT TO BE A PART OF THAT'

THE first confirmed signing of the summer and probably among the most surprising, Andriy Vornonin could prove to be one of the bargains of the season.

The Ukrainian international joined the Reds on a free transfer from Bayer Leverkusen last month after agreeing to the move back in February.

The 27-year-old has spent the past 12 years in the Bundesliga and scored 21 goals in 71 appearances at the Bayer Arena.

It is a record that does not promise an avalanche of goals and there are those who doubt whether he has predatory instinct to be the 15-goal a season man the Reds require.

But that did not deter Rafa Benitez who believes Voronin can offer his side something different and he has high hopes for the player who is set to inherit Luis Garcia's number 10 shirt.

"Voronin is a player with pace and with good movement," said Benitez.

"He plays between the lines, between defenders. He is a good worker also, and he scores goals.

"He has played as a left winger and as a striker on his own last season. I watched some videos of him on the left and on the right, but this is not his position, he is a striker.

"But that means we have another player who has game intelligence and I'm quite sure that will be an advantage."

Voronin, who has already played at Anfield after featuring in Bayer Leverkusen's 3-1 Champions League defeat back in 2005, is delighted to be making the move to Liverpool and while some may question his ability to adapt to the pace of the Premiership, he holds no such fears.

"I played in Germany for over a decade and I've played Champions League football too," he says. "I'm sure all that will help me to find my way.

"It's always been my ambition to play in England, I've thought about it for a long time. "From my point of view it's the strongest, most competitive league there is. Most of the world's best players perform here and it will give me great pleasure to play with and against some of them.

"I first heard about Liverpool's interest from my manager at Leverkusen around the turn of the year. I was very excited and now I am absolutely delighted to be wearing a red shirt today. Hopefully I will have a lot more opportunities to do so."

With competition for places set to be high, the former Borussia Moenchengladbach, Mainz and Cologne forward knows he will have a fight on his hands to land that regular starting berth.

But quality invariably breeds success and he believes Rafa's summer spending spree can only be good for the future.

"These are exciting times at this club," he said. "The run to the Champions League final was excellent, there's a new stadium on the way and of course Fernando Torres has arrived too. I think we've got a lot to look forward to and I want to be a part of that."

adidas
LFC

LUCAS LEIVA

'WHAT I HAVE BEEN OFFERED AND THE TEAM FROM WHICH IT CAME FROM MADE IT IMPOSSIBLE TO SAY NO'

A £5MILLION capture from Gremio, Lucas Pezzini Leiva has all the credentials to be the latest South American star to shine at Anfield.

The 20-year-old midfielder, simply known as 'Lucas,' won the prestigious Golden Boot in his country last season, becoming the youngest ever winner of an award that boasts Zico, Romario and Kaka as some of its previous winners.

His rise and rise in the Brazilian game has seen him captain the country's under-20 side and his arrival will further increase the competition for places in an already congested midfield department that includes Steven Gerrard, Xabi Alonso, Momo Sissoko and Javier Mascherano.

While few Reds fans will have seen the youngster play live, boss Rafa Benitez is convinced he can make a name for himself at Anfield.

"He is a fantastic player for the present and the future," said Rafa.

"He can play as a holding midfielder but he can also get from box to box and so I am looking forward to seeing him score goal for Liverpool in the future.

"A lot of clubs in England and Spain were asking about him but our scouting department has again been working really hard and it's good that he's coming to us."

The youngster, who is the nephew of former Atletico Madrid star Levinha, has made a huge impression in just two seasons with Gremio and has even featured for the senior national team, although the 4-0 friendly win against club side Al-Kuwait in October 2006 is not officially recognised by FIFA.

Last season he starred as he led Gremio to the Copa Libertadores final but it all ended in heartache as they were comprehensively thrashed 5-0 on aggregate by Boca Juniors.

It proved to be his final match with the side nicknamed 'Imortal Tricolor' (immortal of three colours) and

although he is sad to be leaving his homeland at such a young age he is relishing the chance to showcase his skills in the Premiership.

"To tell you the truth, I really didn't expect to leave Brazil so soon," he said. "But what I have been offered and the team from which it came from made it impossible to say no."

'OUR SCOUTING DEPARTMENT HAS AGAIN BEEN WORKING REALLY HARD AND IT'S GOOD THAT HE IS COMING TO US'

NIKOLAY MIHAYLOV

FOLLOWING the departure of Jerzy Dudek and the decision not to make Daniele Padelli's loan move permanent, Rafa Benitez swooped to bolster his goalkeeping options with the addition of Bulgarian under-21 stopper Nikolay Mihaylov.

The 19-year-old, who is the son of Bulgarian football union president Borislav Mihaylov, joins the Reds from Levski Sofia, where he was part of the squad that competed in last season's

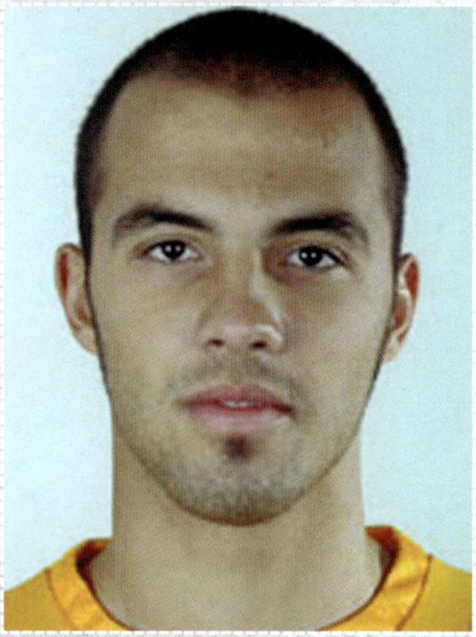

Champions League.

Although he is likely to remain behind Pepe Reina and Scott Carson in the pecking order he has a good pedigree having already represented his country at senior level.

On signing for Liverpool he could not hide his excitement.

"I have no words," he said.

"This is the greatest moment of my life."

'THIS IS THE GREATEST MOMENT OF MY LIFE'

KRISZTIAN NEMETH & ANDRAS SIMON

TWO teenage strikers who have already shown glimpses of their quality with Hungarian international youth teams, Nemeth and Simon have been earmarked as ones for the future by the Liverpool boss.

Nemeth, an 18-year-old striker who signed from MTK Hungaria, scored 14 goals in 34 matches in his first season in the professional game, while his 17-year-old club mate Simon has less experience but has impressed for Hungary's under-17 side.

Benitez has brought them in with the future very much in mind and revealed the Reds had beaten a host of top clubs to their signature.

"We have been watching these players for a long time," he said.

"There were a lot of big clubs interested in them, such as Real Madrid, Ajax and PSV Eindhoven.

"It's never easy for a young player to settle in England, but we know they have outstanding ability."

KRISZTIAN NEMETH (in red)

SEBASTIAN LETO

AN unusually large left winger who stands at six foot two, Leto joined the Reds in January earlier this year, but remained on loan in his native Argentina with Lanus until the end of the season.

The 20-year-old had attracted interest from home and abroad with River Plate and Spanish outfit Real Betis rumoured to be preparing bids.

But while other clubs hesitated the Reds took advantage and swooped in to take him to Anfield.

In two seasons with Lanus he has scored eight goals in 52 matches and is relishing the chance to try his luck in the Premiership.

"I am calm," he said after his £1.8million move was announced.

"Liverpool is a club with a lot of history. I do not fear the challenge."

The day I signed . . .

"It was just meeting him for the first five minutes that persuaded me that he was a good man and Liverpool would be a good club to be with. I couldn't believe it when we were coming down the M6, with vice-chairman Sidney Reaks, who had a Rolls Royce at the time, and me and Bill in the back. I was only 22 and didn't know what to say. Bill just turned round and said: 'Ron, I want you to captain the side. You will be my eyes, my ears and my voice on that pitch.' I thought to myself: 'bloody hell.' It's a big thing at 22, and I'd never ever seen the place. I did that for him, I captained Liverpool for 10 years. It was the best 10 years of my career and my life."

RON YEATS

Big Buys

WHEN THE CLUB HAVE BROKEN THEIR TRANSFER RECORD TO GET THEIR MAN

WHOEVER invented the phrase 'you get what you pay for in this world' certainly wasn't a football manager.

The saying implies that the more you pay for something, the better the quality of your purchase will be.

Anyone involved in football knows that isn't necessarily the case.

Would anyone consider that Newcastle United got a better player when they signed Titus Bramble for £5million than Liverpool did when they brought Sami Hyypia to Anfield for £2.5million?

Does anyone really think Manchester United got two better years of service from Juan Sebastian Veron than Liverpool did from Gary McAllister, despite the fact the Argentinian was brought to Old Trafford for £28million – around £28million more than the Scot cost the Reds?

Market forces sometimes dictate that you have to pay more for a player than you would like to in order to make sure you get your man, but Liverpool's experiences when it comes to breaking their transfer record down the years have been largely positive.

When the Liverpool manager of the day has asked the men that guard the purse strings to splash out to land a big signing, the result has often seen the club get a player who has made a big impact.

There have, of course, been times when big money has been paid and the player brought in has failed to live up to expectations, but that, as they say, is football.

Liverpool first shelled out major cash to land a big signing when Sam Hardy was brought to the club from Chesterfield for £500 in 1905.

Hardy was an international class keeper who went on to play for

I 28803089 A
I 28803089 A
TREASURY SECRETARY

Big Buys

Djibril Cisse, Dean Saunders, Mark Lawrenson, Peter Thompson and John Toshack all arrived at Anfield as club record transfers

England 21 times.

He won the championship in his first season with the club and was a regular between the sticks for six years, before he eventually moved on to Aston Villa. Few people could accuse him of being a flop.

Since his signing near the start of last century, however, the club have never broken their transfer record to land a goalkeeper. This perhaps shows how players of other positions command a larger fee, because no-one could accuse Ray Clemence or Bruce Grobbelaar of not having a lasting and high quality impact during their time at Anfield, despite the fact they were bought for modest fees.

It is strikers that attract the highest prices because they fire the imagination of supporters. What they can bring to a team if they are successful is the most precious commodity in the game – goals.

It is fair to say, however, that some strikers that Liverpool have pushed the boat out to sign have delivered far less than their price tag would suggest they were capable of.

The last player before Fernando Torres to be brought to Anfield for a record fee was Djibril Cisse.

Gerard Houllier had worked for years to secure the signature of the French striker and spent £14.5million of the club's money to make it happen.

The summer Cisse eventually arrived coincided with Houllier leaving the club and the pair never had the chance to work together – and it's probably fair to say that the eccentric goalscorer didn't really fit into the plans of new manager Rafael Benitez.

After three seasons with the club, one broken leg, two major winners medals and one season on loan, Cisse left the club to join Marseille having failed to justify a hefty price tag.

The two players that preceded Cisse as strikers who the club had to break the bank to buy also had a mixed time at Anfield and left the club with fans wondering whether things could have worked out differently.

Emile Heskey signed for Liverpool from Leicester City for £11million in 2000 having shown great potential as a player with all the tools to be a big hit with a top four side and the national team.

His first full season with Liverpool

Kenny Dalglish more than doubled the club record transfer fee when he arrived in 1977

Sam Hardy joined the club for £500 in 1905

The day I signed . . .

"As a kid, I was always watching Liverpool on television in the great times of the Eighties. So I was very honoured when I got an offer from them and I didn't have to think much about it, I just signed.

"It was always a dream for me to play in England. I never thought about Spain or Italy. It was mainly the tremendous atmosphere I wanted to experience. I had a taste of it in Euro '96 when I was over here with Germany, and the German players who have played in England always came back and told us amazing stories about the crowds and the buzz you get in the stadiums."

MARKUS BABBEL

yielded 22 goals and three winners medals, but that was as good as it got for the man with the middle name Ivanhoe.

He ultimately left the club to join Birmingham City in 2004 having scored little better than a goal every four games – not enough for a man every fan knew was capable of more.

One of the most anticipated signings in Liverpool's history came when Stan Collymore arrived for a British transfer record of £8.5million in 1995.

He lasted only two seasons with the club and won no medals, but struck up an awesome strike partnership with Robbie Fowler that had fans purring. He was another player who was capable of a long and successful career at the club if only things had worked out differently.

Other strikers who arrived with a fanfare but failed to win a place in the fans' hearts included Tony Hateley, Dean Saunders and Alun Evans.

But for every failure, there has been a success and no-one could accuse Ian St John, Kenny Dalglish, John Toshack or Peter Beardsley of letting down the manager who had shown huge faith in them.

All of them were bought for huge fees and had already established themselves as players of great talent, and all proved more than capable of showcasing their abilities on the biggest stage when the pressure was on.

Even the managers of the past could spot a good centre-forward when they saw one.

George Patterson signed Jim Smith from Ayr United for £5,500 in 1929, but despite the fact the striker was in and out of the side for three years, nobody could complain at a goal return of 38 goals in 62 matches.

Patterson also signed Sam English from Glasgow Rangers in 1933 for £8,000 – another striker who didn't feature in every game but still came up with 26 goals in 50 games over two seasons.

Albert Stubbins became an icon on

Merseyside, having joined the club on the toss of a coin after Everton showed interest in him too.

He was brought from Newcastle for £13,000 straight after the second world war and played a huge part in the club winning the title in his first season.

Big signings aren't exclusively about strikers though and special players have demanded special fees through the years.

Tom Bradshaw arrived from Bury in 1930 and played either wing-half of centre-half over eight years with the club after signing for £8,000.

Peter Thompson was an iconic winger that was a real favourite with Shankly.

The Reds won the race to sign him for a club record £37,000 in 1963 and it proved to be a bargain as he tormented full-backs for over a decade in the red of Liverpool.

Four years later and Shankly took a chance on a Blackpool youngster by the name of Emlyn Hughes – not that the great Scot ever considered it a gamble – and the £65,000 he paid was made to look like small change as he went on to captain the club to successes at home and in Europe.

He was one player that proved the phrase 'you get what you pay for in this world' definitely can be very misleading.

Sometimes you get an awful lot more than you pay for . . . and if our latest record breaker Torres can be half as successful as Crazy Horse was it will be £20million well spent.

Tom Bradshaw joined the Reds from Bury in 1930 and went on to play nearly 300 games for the club

David Johnson chats with Kevin Keegan after arriving from Ipswich in August 1976, while Kevin Lewis shakes hands with Liverpool chairman TV Williams after signing from Sheffield United in 1960

THE MEN THE REDS HAVE BROKEN A CLUB RECORD TO BUY . . .

	DATE	BOUGHT FROM	FEE
SAM HARDY	MAY 1905	CHESTERFIELD	£500
FRED HOPKIN	MAY 1921	MANCHESTER U	£2,800
TOM MORRISON	NOV 1927	ST MIRREN	£4,000
JIM SMITH	SEP 1929	AYR UNITED	£5,500
TOM BRADSHAW	JAN 1930	BURY	£8,000
SAM ENGLISH	AUG 1933	GLASGOW RANGERS	£8,000*
MATT BUSBY	MAR 1936	MANCHESTER C	£8,000
ALBERT STUBBINS	SEP 1946	NEWCASTLE	£13,000
KEVIN LEWIS	JUN 1960	SHEFFIELD U	£13,000
GORDON MILNE	AUG 1960	PRESTON	£16,000
IAN ST JOHN	MAY 1961	MOTHERWELL	£35,000
PETER THOMPSON	AUG 1963	PRESTON	£37,000
GEOFF STRONG	NOV 1964	ARSENAL	£40,000
EMLYN HUGHES	FEB 1967	BLACKPOOL	£65,000
TONY HATELEY	JUN 1967	CHELSEA	£96,000
ALUN EVANS	SEP 1968	WOLVERHAMPTON	£100,000
JOHN TOSHACK	NOV 1970	CARDIFF C	£110,000
PETER CORMACK	JUL 1972	NOTTINGHAM FOREST	£110,000
RAY KENNEDY	JUL 1974	ARSENAL	£180,000
DAVID JOHNSON	AUG 1976	IPSWICH T	£200,000
KENNY DALGLISH	AUG 1977	CELTIC	£440,000
CRAIG JOHNSTON	APR 1981	MIDDLESBROUGH	£575,000
MARK LAWRENSON	AUG 1981	BRIGHTON	£900,000
PETER BEARDSLEY	JUL 1987	NEWCASTLE U	£1,900,000
IAN RUSH	AUG 1988	JUVENTUS	£2,800,000
DEAN SAUNDERS	JUL 1991	DERBY C	£2,900,000
PHIL BABB	SEP 1994	COVENTRY C	£3,600,000
STAN COLLYMORE	JUL 1995	NOTTINGHAM FOREST	£8,500,000
EMILE HESKEY	MAR 2000	LEICESTER C	£11,000,000
DJIBRIL CISSE	JUL 2004	AUXERRE	£14,500,000
FERNANDO TORRES	JUL 2007	ATLETICO MADRID	£20,000,000

* AN APPROXIMATE AMOUNT

Bill Shankly signed Tony Hateley for £96,000 but sold him to Coventry just over a year later

Stan Collymore's move to Liverpool for £8.5m in 1995 was a British transfer record fee

Gambles that didn't pay off: El-Hadji Diouf, Djibril Cisse, Bernard Diomede and

IN the world of a football manager there is no escaping the bitter taste associated with a bad signing.

It is inevitable and something even the greatest have been unable to avoid.

Bill Nicholson, Matt Busby, Bill Shankly, Jock Stein and Bob Paisley lead the way as the finest managers these shores have ever seen and yet all have been stung in the transfer market at one time or another.

Shanks was hailed as the messiah and he proved he had the golden touch by bringing in the giant presence of Ron Yeats, the inspirational passion of Emlyn Hughes and the goalscoring genius of Kevin Keegan.

But for every Ian St John there would still be the rare error of judgement that introduced the Kop to a Stephen Arnold.

A £12,000 signing from Crewe, Arnold made just one appearance for the Reds when Shankly opted to field an under strength side for the final league match of the 1970/71 season.

It was the highlight of his career as he left Liverpool within two years of signing and retired from professional football at the age of 23.

To be fair Arnold was not alone and his name sits alongside Frank McGarvey, Jack Whitham and Peter Spiring as players who failed to make an impact at Shankly's Liverpool.

Of course, nowadays the multi-million pound nature of the market makes the pitfalls of a poor signing all the more disastrous and although Bob Paisley, Kenny Dalglish, Graeme Souness and Roy Evans were all guilty of wasting

The ones that didn't work out

WHEN BIG SIGNINGS GO WRONG

Games forwards have played before their first Liverpool goal

Player	Minutes	Games	Debut goal
1 Peter Crouch	1,228	18	03.12.2005
2 Arthur Rowley	1,019	11	No goal
3 Ian Rush	813	10	30.09.1981
4 Michael Robinson	784	10	28.09.1983
5 Jack Balmer	531	6	07.12.1935
6 Kevin Baron	527	6	08.11.1947
7 Phil Boersma	480	7	04.11.1970
8 Emile Heskey	436	5	01.04.2000
9 Les Shannon	382	5	30.08.1948
10 Alf Arrowsmith	361	5	16.09.1963

The proof that tables DO lie

THIS table would suggest that Peter Crouch and Ian Rush are among the worst three forwards in Liverpool history. Not too many fans would agree with that.

Christian Ziege (left) could be described as expensive mistakes

what we perceive to be our hard-earned cash, it is Gerard Houllier who is most famous for bringing in duds for big money.

The £5million we shelled out on Middlesbrough's German international Christian Ziege looked to be good business for a player who had proved himself in the Premiership.

But his defensive deficiencies were too often exposed and he rarely produced the performances to justify the controversial circumstances in which he arrived.

And what about World Cup winner Bernard Diomede?

The Frenchman turned up at Anfield amidst high expectation following his £3million move from Auxerre but made just five appearances and is best remembered for an overhead kick in a match at home to Sunderland that was adjudged not to have crossed the goalline.

However, the disappointments of Diomede, Jean Michel Ferri and Djimi Traore did not seem to deter Houllier from continually raiding the French market and Bruno Cheyrou, El-Hadji Diouf, Salif Diao, Djibril Cisse and the 'gems' Florent Sinama-Pongolle and Anthony Le Tallec, all arrived for a combined total of more than £35million.

The fact the club have struggled to recoup less than a third of that outlay suggests just how much these players flopped at Anfield and proves that money helps, but it doesn't always buy success.

Even the best make mistakes: Bill Shankly signed (top to bottom) Stephen Arnold, Frank McGarvey, Jack Whitham and Peter Spiring, but none of those players left a great impression on the history of Liverpool FC

Hits & misses

Signed by Rafael Benitez

THREE OF THE BEST, THREE OF THE WORST

AFTER inheriting a squad top heavy with average players, Rafa Benitez soon found out that he did not have the funds available to indulge in the major surgery necessary to transform Liverpool back into English football's most dominant force.

He spent his first pre-season assessing the level of Gerard Houllier's legacy and when he did finally opt to delve into the transfer market he stuck to what he knew best, predominantly signing Spanish players.

Indeed, his first six acquisitions all arrived from his homeland but for all the success of the likes of Xabi Alonso and Luis Garcia, there were the disappointments of Mauricio Pellegrino and Fernando Morientes.

But to his great credit, Rafa has always acknowledged his mistakes and swiftly removed any dead wood – something Antonio Nunez, Josemi, Jan Kromkamp and Pellegrino all found to their cost.

It is evidence of the ruthless streak within a manager with a mentality focused on winning trophies.

The free transfer signing of Liverpool legend Robbie Fowler was seen by some cynics as a way of appeasing Reds fans for an inability to mount a serious Premiership challenge, but he has also released the likes of Vladimir Smicer, Milan Baros and Djimi Traore despite their role in our 2005 Champions League triumph.

With Rafa there is no room for sentiment and when he felt Fowler was surplus to requirements at the end of last season he made the decision to let him go with his head and not his heart.

Since his first season he has continued to acquire players from Spain, but has also begun to understand the English market and with limited funds available he has made the best of his situation by landing players with potential, such as Jermaine Pennant, rather than the established stars.

Time will tell just how successful Rafa's track record in the transfer market as Liverpool manager will be, but there is no doubt that with the likes of Xabi Alonso, Daniel Agger, Pepe Reina and Javier Mascherano he has already struck gold.

*** To date (23 July 07) Benitez has bought 44 players for a total of £125,096,000 but due to the limited transfer funds at his disposal he has also sold 45 players for £62,175,000.**

adidas
MASCHERANO
20
Carlsberg

DANIEL AGGER

THE fact Agger, 22, has been compared with the likes of Alan Hansen and Mark Lawrenson after less than two seasons at Anfield shows just how big an impression he has made since moving to the Reds in January 2006.

A £5.8million buy from Brondby, Agger first emerged as one of Rafa Benitez's top transfer targets when he starred for Denmark during an emphatic 4-1 win over England in August 2005.

The Dane has excelled alongside Jamie Carragher and has even developed a reputation for some sensational shooting with spectacular goals against West Ham and Chelsea – in the Champions League semi-final – the pick of the bunch.

HITS

XABI ALONSO

ALONSO first caught the eye when he played a starring role in Real Sociedad's surprise challenge for the La Liga title back in the 2002/03 season.

His vision and ability to spray raking balls to feet soon had some of Europe's top clubs taking notice and it was inevitable that he would move on to bigger and better things.

Somewhat surprisingly however, it wasn't a move to the Real Madrids or Barcelonas of this world that interested him the most.

Instead he opted to leave his homeland behind and join his compatriot Benitez in trying to re-invigorate a flagging Liverpool side.

While some players take time to adapt to the English game, Xabi found his feet immediately and he has already scored two goals from inside his own half as testament to his outstanding vision.

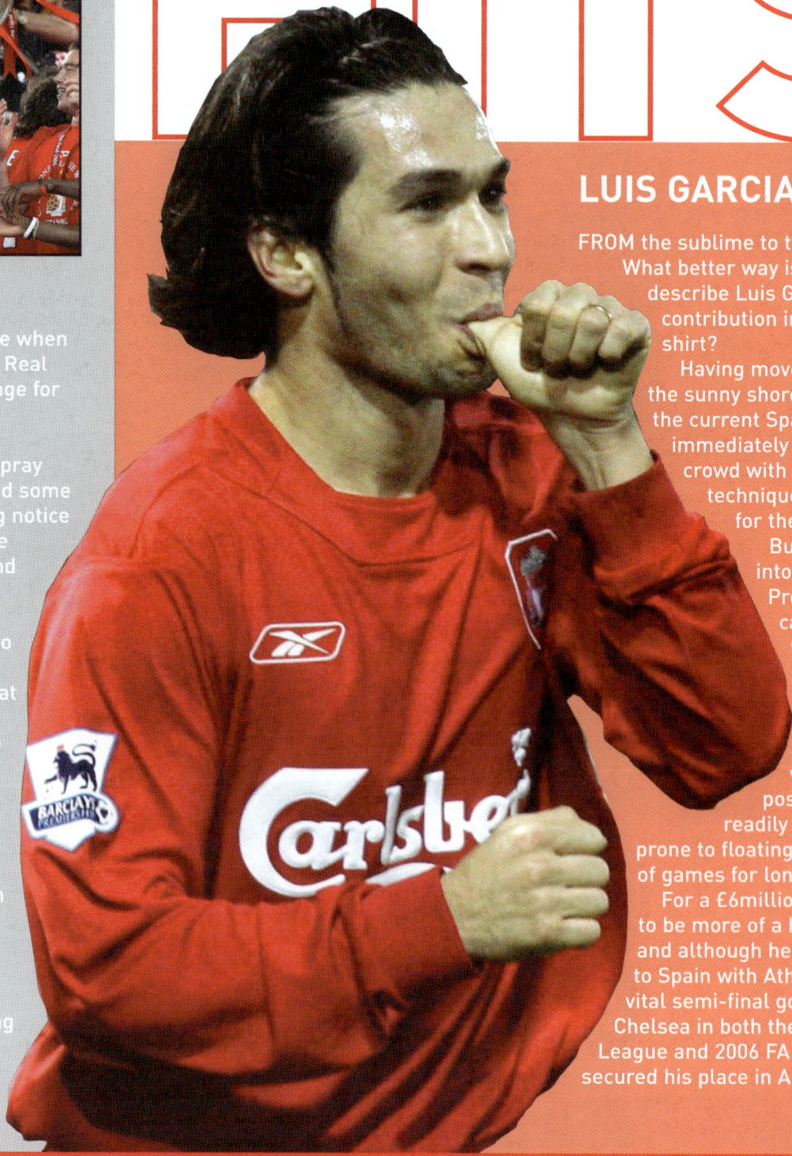

LUIS GARCIA

FROM the sublime to the ridiculous. What better way is there to describe Luis Garcia's contribution in a Liverpool shirt?

Having moved to Anfield from the sunny shores of Barcelona the current Spain international immediately wowed the Reds crowd with his tremendous technique and penchant for the dramatic.

But as he settled into life in the Premiership we came to realise that for all the extravagance and genius there is a frustrating side to him that wastes possession far too readily and he is also prone to floating on the periphery of games for long spells.

For a £6million buy he proved to be more of a hit than a miss and although he has now returned to Spain with Athletico Madrid, his vital semi-final goals against Chelsea in both the 2005 Champions League and 2006 FA Cup, have secured his place in Anfield folklore.

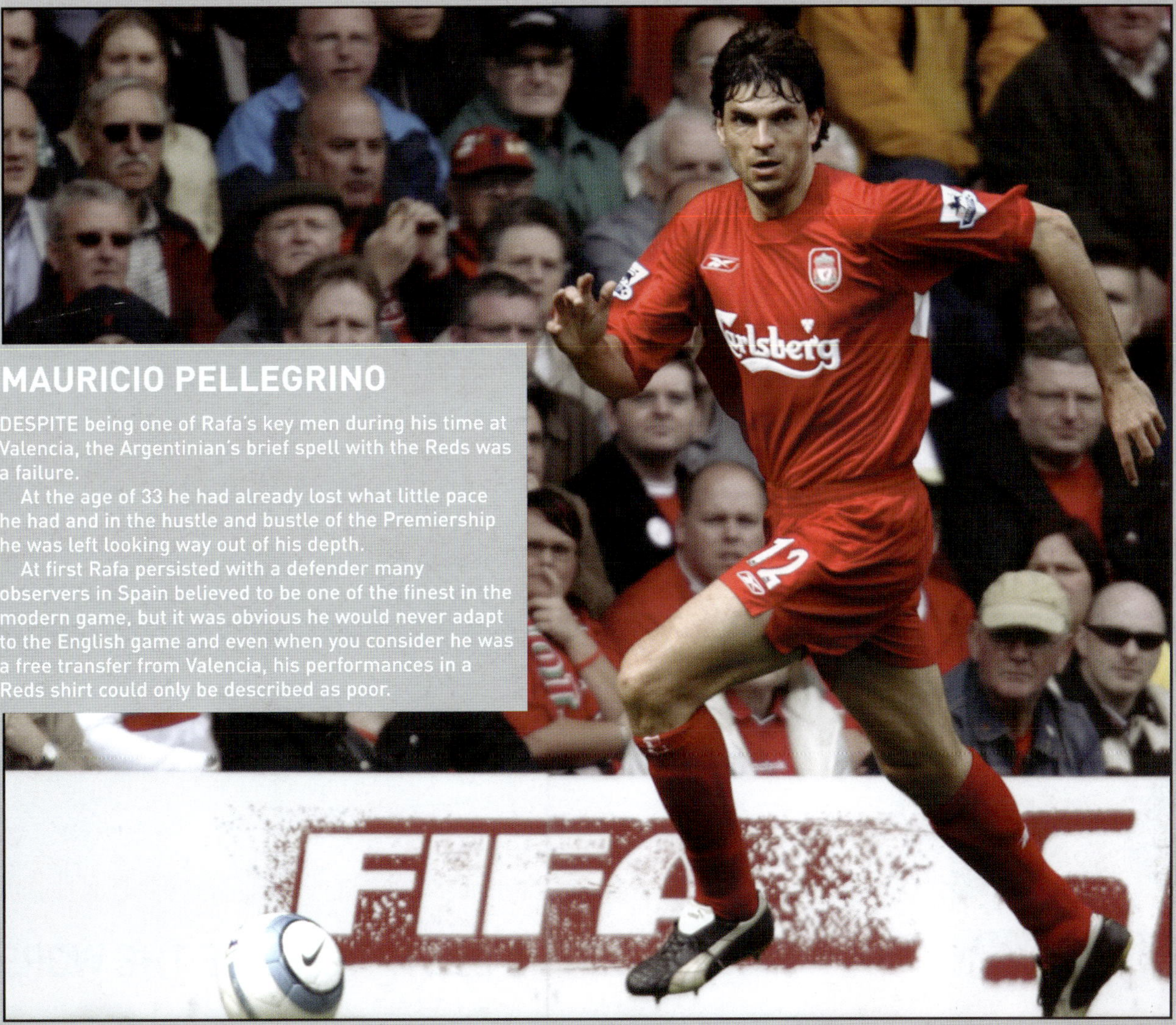

MAURICIO PELLEGRINO

DESPITE being one of Rafa's key men during his time at Valencia, the Argentinian's brief spell with the Reds was a failure.

At the age of 33 he had already lost what little pace he had and in the hustle and bustle of the Premiership he was left looking way out of his depth.

At first Rafa persisted with a defender many observers in Spain believed to be one of the finest in the modern game, but it was obvious he would never adapt to the English game and even when you consider he was a free transfer from Valencia, his performances in a Reds shirt could only be described as poor.

MISSES

FERNANDO MORIENTES

A TALENTED targetman who had starred for both Real Madrid and Spain, Morientes was earmarked by Benitez as the top class striker capable of taking Liverpool to the next level.

Having finished the previous campaign as the Champions League top scorer with Monaco, his £6.3million move to the Premiership looked set to be one of the bargain transfers of the season.

But try as he might, it never quite happened for Mori at Anfield.

A regular goalscorer throughout his career he struggled to adapt to the pace of the Premiership and was troubled by a succession of injuries that prevented him from putting a goalscoring run together.

In fact he looked distinctly average and immobile for the majority of his 61 appearances for Liverpool, hitting a measly return of just 12 goals.

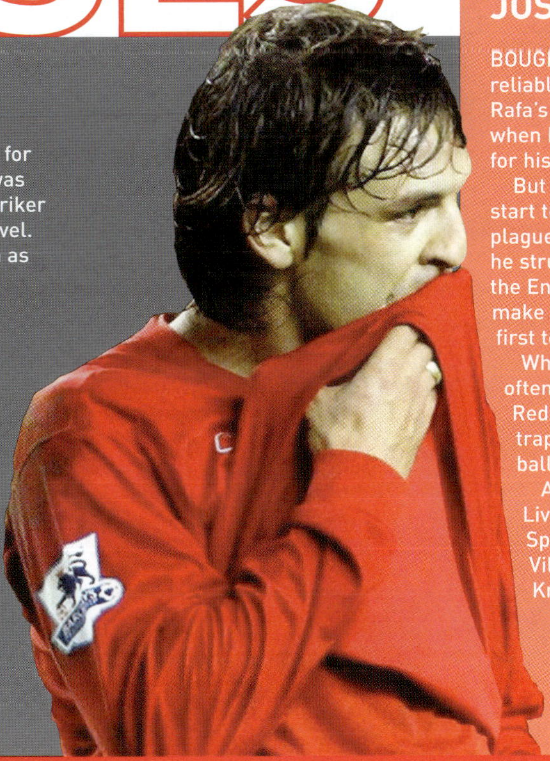

JOSEMI

BOUGHT as cover for the ever-reliable Steve Finnan, Josemi was Rafa's first signing for the Reds when Rafa paid Malaga £2million for his services.

But although he made a decent start to his Liverpool career, he was plagued by niggling injuries and as he struggled to come to terms with the English language he failed to make a lasting impression on the first team.

When he was selected he was often caught napping when the Reds tried to deploy the offside trap and was guilty of giving the ball away far too cheaply.

After just 35 appearances for Liverpool he moved back to Spain as part of deal with Villarreal that saw Jan Kromkamp move to Anfield.

Hits & misses

Signed by Gerard Houllier

THREE OF THE BEST, THREE OF THE WORST

THE summer of 1999 marked the first phase of Gerard Houllier's French revolution.

Looking ahead to his first full season in sole charge of the Reds he raided the transfer market on no fewer than seven occasions in an attempt to revamp what had become a struggling Reds side.

The pick of the new boys were Sami Hyypia, Stephane Henchoz, Dietmar Hamann and Titi Camara, who all enjoyed impressive debut seasons and were unlucky not to help the club secure a Champions League place.

Further success in the transfer market followed a year later when the acquisition of Gary McAllister, Markus Babbel, Jari Litmanen and Nick Barmby bolstered the Reds' squad and saw us clinch a unique cup treble.

It wasn't all plain sailing in the transfer market though.

To say that all of Houllier's signings had been a success would have been wrong, as the likes of Pegguy Arphexad, Christian Ziege, Frode Kippe and Jean Michel Ferri are evidence of.

But up until the end of the 2002/03 season he seemed to know what he was doing and the players he signed had shown some sort of talent, even if they had not reached the level required to play for Liverpool.

However, the summer of 2002 saw the Frenchman go some way to ending his hopes of taking Liverpool to the holy grail of the Premiership trophy.

Had his illness affected his judgment? Only he will know the answer to that, but he certainly did his best to blow up to £20million on players who were no better than the ones he already had in his squad.

A staggering fee of £10million brought the foul tempered El-Hadji Diouf to the club, while £4million captured Bruno Cheyrou – the most un-Zidane-like player in France.

The rest of the kitty saw us waste £5.5million to secure the services of the mediocre Salif Diao.

His final act as boss in the transfer market summed it up when he broke the Reds' transfer record to pay £14.5million for Djibril Cisse – another Frenchman who had still to prove his top class pedigree.

*** Gerard Houllier spent £125.4million on 40 players. He also sold 48 players for £60.675million**

LIVERPOOL
FOOTBALL CLUB

MARKUS BABBEL

THE Reds were made to wait for Markus Babbel but when he finally arrived from Bayern Munich on a free transfer he was worth the patience.

His impact at right-back during the treble season was a throwback to the days of Phil Neal and Alan Kennedy when the Reds' full-backs surged forward and chipped in with their fair share of goals.

Indeed, Babbel scored six goals that season, including a strike against Everton in the remarkable 3-2 win at Goodison Park and the opener in the UEFA Cup final in Dortmund.

Sadly for Markus and Liverpool, he was struck down by a rare condition called Guillain-Barre Syndrome and was ruled out of action for over a year.

When he returned he was a shadow of his former self and was never able to recapture the form that had made him such a fans favourite and was eventually released by Houllier.

SAMI HYYPIA

IF you were running a poll of Gerard Houllier's best signing, Sami Hyypia would probably finish a clear winner.

Regarded as a relative unknown throughout Europe, Hyypia had just captained unfancied Dutch outfit Willem II to a Champions League place when the Reds came calling.

For many fans it was a puzzling transfer, but within a few weeks of the start of the season the fans knew they had a superb centre-back at the club.

Immaculate positioning, towering ability in the air and a super reader of the game, it is easy to see why so many former Reds have labelled him the modern day Ron Yeats.

After captaining the side to countless cup successes he has proved to be an astonishing bargain at £2.5million and he will go down as one of the finest defenders to have ever graced the Anfield turf.

HITS

DIETMAR HAMANN

ONE of the finest holding midfielders of his generation, it says a lot about Didi Hamann's impact at the club that you look at an £8million price tag and think it was money well spent.

The German arrived at the club in the summer of 1999 and proved to be the perfect shield in front of the highly praised centre-back partnership of Sami Hyypia and Stephane Henchoz.

At first Hamann was a player who took more plaudits from his team-mates than from the fans, but it soon became evident to everyone that Liverpool's defensive frailties were exposed far more frequently when the German with a scouse accent was not on the teamsheet.

No match highlighted this more than the 2005 Champions League final when he came on to the field with the Reds 3-0 down and played a pivotal role in helping Liverpool come back from the dead to win on penalties.

MISSES

FRODE KIPPE

WHEN Gerard Houllier followed up the signing of Jean Michel Ferri with this Norwegian misfit he must have thought he'd been given a red herring rather than a 'Kippe.'

The young defender joined Liverpool from Lillestrom for £700,000 but his lack of pace and poor ability on the ball led to some of his team-mates identifying him as the worst player they had ever seen at Liverpool.

It was hardly the confidence boost he needed and after making just two Reds appearances he moved to Stoke City on loan for two seasons before returning to Lillestrom when his contract expired.

SALIF DIAO

A POWERFUL midfielder who lacked overall technique and had a habit of committing rash tackles, Diao was one of a trio of transfer mistakes made by Houllier in the summer of 2002.

The midfielder had impressed for Senegal in the 2002 World Cup finals and despite having Steven Gerrard, Dietmar Hamann, Danny Murphy and Igor Biscan at the club, Houllier decided he needed yet another central midfielder.

The Frenchman claimed he had signed the new Patrick Vieira when he made obscure French club Sedan's day by handing them £4.7million for Diao.

After less than a month with the Reds it became clear Diao had nothing in common with Vieira other than the fact they both picked up their fair share of bookings.

The Reds knew they had paid well over the odds for such an average midfield man and despite loan spells at Birmingham, Portsmouth and Stoke, he hung on to his Anfield dream until his contract finally ran out in January 2007.

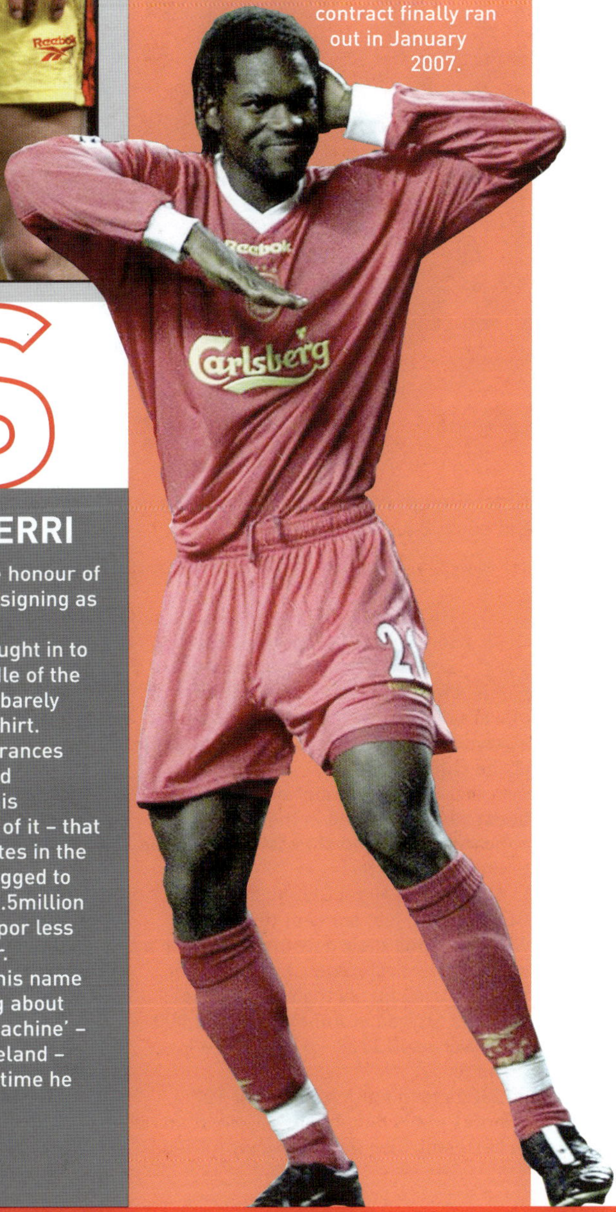

JEAN MICHEL FERRI

JEAN MICHEL FERRI has the honour of being Gerard Houllier's first signing as Reds boss.

The midfield man was brought in to add further steel to the middle of the park, but as it turned out he barely kicked a ball in a Liverpool shirt.

He made substitute appearances against Chelsea and Sheffield Wednesday, but such was his influence – or indeed lack of it – that he managed just 50 minutes in the red shirt before being flogged to Sochaux for the same £1.5million we had paid to Istanbulspor less than nine months earlier.

With five France caps to his name he must have had something about him but unfortunately 'the machine' – as he was known in his homeland – had developed a fault by the time he arrived at Anfield.

Debut DAZZLERS

Nigel Clough powers in his first league goal for Liverpool against Sheffield Wednesday at Anfield in 1993. He went on to score the second as well in a 2-0 win

WHAT better way to endear yourself to your new supporters than by scoring a goal on your debut?

It is a feat no fewer than 86 Liverpool players have achieved and yet it has not always been a marker for future success at the club.

In fact a large number of those who can boast having notched in their first appearance in a red shirt failed to live up to their dream start.

Alun Evans, Nigel Clough and Mark Gonzalez are just some of the players who rewarded their new manager with a goal in their first match, but who later failed to truly justify their transfer fee.

Evans arrived at Anfield for £100,000 from Wolves in 1968 – a record fee for a teenager.

But despite netting after just 10 minutes of his debut in a 4-0 win at home to Leicester City, he never truly fulfilled his potential at Liverpool and lasted just four seasons, playing 111 games and scoring 33 goals.

Bobby Graham was another forward who announced himself to the Merseyside public in dramatic fashion.

He started off with a debut strike in a 6-1 win over KR Reykjavik in a European Cup preliminary round fixture in 1964 before netting a hat-trick in a 5-1 triumph over Aston Villa on his league debut a fortnight later.

But unfortunately for Graham he could not maintain such a prolific strike rate and he failed to command a regular place in the side until the 1969/70 season when he hit 21 goals in 57 matches.

However, it all turned pear-shaped when he broke his leg in a match at home to Chelsea and in 1972 he joined Coventry City having struggled to recapture the form that he had enjoyed when he broke into the side at the age of 19.

Fast-forwarding to 1993 and after what felt like an eternity it seemed as though Liverpool had found a new number seven to follow in the footsteps of Keegan and Dalglish.

Nigel Clough had been a thorn in Liverpool's side throughout his time with Nottingham Forest and when he moved from the City Ground for £2.275million he was tipped to lead the Reds' bid to reclaim their crown as England's top side.

Two goals on his league debut in a 2-0 win over Sheffield Wednesday was the perfect start but it would prove to be one of the few highlights for Cloughie.

The player many observers had hailed as a man born to play the Liverpool way failed to reproduce his Nottingham Forest form at Anfield and a series of disappointing performances saw him dropped to the substitutes bench and he

Gabriel Paletta got his first chance to show what he could do in a Carling Cup tie against Reading in 2006 and promptly headed in a goal to be the last Reds player to score on his debut

New Chilean signing Mark Gonzalez had only been on the pitch a few minutes in a Champions League qualifier against Maccabi Haifa when he slotted in this late winner in 2006

After failing to score in 49 matches for Everton, Abel Xavier joined the Reds and scored after 16 minutes of his debut against Ipswich in 2002

Titi Camara arrived as something of an unknown quantity when he joined the Reds from Marseille in 1999, but he announced himself in the best way possible with a winner at Sheffield Wednesday

played just 44 games before being sold to Manchester City in January 1996.

Clough's departure was hastened by the British record transfer of Stan Collymore who announced himself to the Liverpool public in sensational fashion when he curled home a brilliant 30-yard winner to give the Reds an opening day win over Sheffield Wednesday in 1995.

Unfortunately for Stan it would be his off-the-field issues that would cast a dark cloud over his career as a Liverpool player.

Four years later and Sheffield Wednesday were again the victims of a Liverpool debutant when little known Guinean forward Titi Camara struck the winner in a 2-1 win at Hillsborough – a match which saw no fewer than six players make their bow in Gerard Houllier's new-look Liverpool side.

However, Camara's inconsistency

Debut DAZZLERS

Alun Evans had a lot of weight on young shoulders when he arrived at Anfield as the country's most expensive teenager, but he made the best possible start to his Liverpool career by scoring on his debut against Leicester

meant he lasted just one season at Anfield as Gerard Houllier looked to turn Liverpool into serious Premiership title contenders.

But for all the misfits and unlucky starlets who endured a difficult time at Anfield, there have also been those who got off the mark and never looked back.

On September 9, 1959, a young man by the name of Roger Hunt came into the side for a second division clash with Scunthorpe at Anfield and promptly gave fans a taster of what was to come.

With the Reds leading 1-0, Hunt secured victory in the 64th minute when he fired home a shot from outside the area that flew in off the underside of the crossbar.

It was the first of 286 goals in 492 matches for the Reds, a strike rate that marks him out as an icon of the Bill Shankly era at Liverpool.

Other new signings who scored on their debuts and went on to enjoy the adulation of the Kop include Kevin Keegan, Billy Liddell, Ronnie Whelan and Ray Kennedy – proving that some players can live up to their early promise.

Since the Millennium just four players have struck goals for the Reds on their full debut.

Craig Bellamy and Mark Gonzalez both got off the mark in a 2-1 win over Maccabi Haifa in a Champions League qualifier last season, but perhaps most surprising was Abel Xavier's deflected effort in a 6-0 win over Ipswich at Portman Road in February 2002.

The last player to score on his Reds bow was Argentinian defender Gabriel Paletta, who headed home at the Kop end during the rollercoaster 4-3 League Cup victory over Reading in October 2006.

Hopefully that will all change at Villa Park on August 11 . . .

FOR ALL THE MISFITS AND UNLUCKY STARLETS WHO ENDURED A DIFFICULT TIME AT ANFIELD, THERE HAVE ALSO BEEN THOSE WHO GOT OFF THE MARK AND NEVER LOOKED BACK

The day I signed . . .

"I'd probably decided to sign for Liverpool even before I met Kenny Dalglish. Newcastle had made it clear they wanted me to go and no other club had come in with a firm offer. Kenny Dalglish wanted to sign good players and build a great team. A few weeks earlier Liverpool had bought John Barnes from Watford and I fancied the idea of playing alongside him. They had also signed John Aldridge from Oxford and I knew he was a reliable goalscorer. They received a lot of money for Ian Rush but were prepared to spend it to achieve success. The talks went so smoothly that we agreed terms within an hour."

PETER BEARDSLEY

REDS' DEBUT GOALSCORERS

Bobby Graham made one of the most explosive league debuts in Liverpool history when he scored a hat-trick against Aston Villa in 1964. This came 12 days after a European debut goal against KR Reykjavik

Stan Collymore was a British transfer record when he signed from Nottingham Forest and all eyes were on him as he scored a winner on his debut against Sheffield Wednesday in 1995

Malcolm McVean	03.09.1892	Hr Walton
John Smith	03.09.1892	Hr Walton
J Cameron	03.09.1892	Hr Walton
James McBride	03.09.1892	Hr Walton
Joe McQue	03.09.1892	Hr Walton
Hugh McQueen	29.10.1892	Newtown
David Henderson	23.09.1893	S Heath
Thomas Bradshaw	28.10.1893	W Arsenal
Arthur Worgan	03.03.1894	Burton S
John Givens	17.03.1894	Lincoln C
Jimmy Ross	13.09.1894	Bolton W
Frank Becton	25.03.1895	Sundland
Ben Bull	25.01.1896	Lincoln C
William Walker	04.09.1897	Stoke C
Joe Lumsden	27.11.1897	N Forest
Jack Cox	12.03.1898	Notts C
Tom Robertson	11.04.1898	Wednesday
John Hunter	02.09.1899	Stoke C
William White	14.09.1901	Everton
George Livingstone	06.09.1902	Blackburn
Sydney Smith	05.09.1903	N Forest
Jack Parkinson	03.10.1903	S Heath
Bill McPherson	06.10.1906	W Arsenal
Charles Hewitt	02.09.1907	N Forest
Harold Fitzpatrick	12.10.1907	Sundland
Ronald Orr	04.04.1908	Aston Villa
Samual Gilligan	24.09.1910	Man City
William Stuart	06.01.1912	Man City
Tom Gracie	24.02.1912	Bury
John Tosswill	04.09.1912	Oldham
Robert McDougall	24.01.1914	WBA
William Banks	14.03.1914	Burnley
Fred Pagnam	10.10.1914	Chelsea
Albert Pearson	30.08.1919	Bradford C
Harry Chambers	30.08.1919	Bradford C
Harry Lewis	30.08.1919	Bradford C
Peter McKinney	09.10.1920	Sheffield U
Jimmy Walsh	29.08.1923	Birm C
Tom Reid	01.05.1926	Sheffield U
William Devlin	07.05.1927	West Ham
Henry Race	15.02.1928	Derby C
Billy Millar	25.08.1928	Bury
Albert Whitehurst	25.08.1928	Bury
Jim Smith	21.09.1929	Man United
Robert Savage	26.09.1931	Grimsby T
Edmund Crawford	27.08.1932	Wolves
Rob Glassey	07.12.1935	Preston
Phil Taylor	28.03.1936	Derby C
Ted Harston	28.08.1937	Chelsea
Jimmy McInnes	19.03.1938	Brentford
Ron Jones	26.03.1938	Man City
Cyril Done	02.09.1939	Chelsea
Billy Liddell	05.01.1946	Chester
Len Carney	31.08.1946	Sheffield U
Albert Stubbins	14.09.1946	Bolton W
William Watkinson	26.04.1947	Aston Villa
John Smith	29.09.1951	Derby C
Brian Jackson	10.11.1951	Bolton W
Alan Arnell	05.12.1953	Blackpool
Tony Rowley	19.04.1954	Middlesbro
Jimmy Melia	17.12.1955	N Forest
Tony McNamara	21.12.1957	Bristol C
Alan Banks	03.09.1958	Brighton
Roger Hunt	09.09.1959	Scunthorpe
Dave Hickson	07.11.1959	Aston Villa
Kevin Lewis	20.08.1960	Leeds U
Bobby Graham	14.09.1964	Reykjavík
John Sealey	26.04.1965	Wolves
Alun Evans	21.09.1968	Leicester
Alec Lindsay	16.09.1969	Dundalk
Kevin Keegan	14.08.1971	N Forest
Ray Kennedy	31.08.1974	Chelsea
Sammy Lee	08.04.1978	Leicester
Ronnie Whelan	03.04.1981	Stoke C
John Wark	31.03.1984	Watford
David Speedie	03.02.1991	Man United
Nigel Clough	14.08.1993	Sheffield W
Robbie Fowler	22.09.1993	Fulham
Stan Collymore	19.08.1995	Sheffield W
Michael Owen	06.05.1997	Wimbledon
Titi Camara	07.08.1999	Sheffield W
Leyton Maxwell	21.09.1999	Hull City
Abel Xavier	09.02.2002	Ipswich T
Craig Bellamy	09.08.2006	Mac Haifa
Mark Gonzalez	09.08.2006	Mac Haifa
Gabriel Paletta	25.10.2006	Reading

BARGAIN HUNT

WHILE FANS NORMALLY WANT THEIR CLUB TO SPLASH THE CASH, THESE MEN SHOW YOU

IT is a major misconception that top money ensures you are buying top quality. Just ask Chelsea and Manchester United.

Alex Ferguson has had his fingers burnt on a number of occasions with the likes of Juan Sebastian Veron and Diego Forlan while Jose Mourinho has yet to see Andriy Shevchenko set the world alight.

The Reds cannot claim to have escaped the pain of big money flops either and the names of Djibril Cisse, El-Hadji Diouf and Emile Heskey still bring a grimace to the faces of most Kopites when the size of their transfer fees are mentioned.

It can happen to all teams and so when a manager is lucky enough to uncover a gem from obscurity or take a gamble on a player that truly pays off it is a sweet moment.

The Bill Shanklys and Bob Paisleys of this world had an uncanny knack for signing unknowns that became household names while for all Gerard Houllier's errors in the transfer market, he was also capable of inspired moments.

But who have stood out as some of the finest bargains in Liverpool's history?

Well, Roger Hunt would certainly be a contender.

Signed from Mid Cheshire League outfit Stockton Heath in the summer of 1958, Hunt made his debut a year later and soon established himself as a regular.

'Sir' Roger is Liverpool's all-time league top goalscorer who won countless honours with Bill Shankly's team and helped England claim the 1966 World Cup – not bad for a player signed for free.

Or what about when the great Scot paid just £18,000 to Scunthorpe in 1966 for Ray Clemence, a raw youngster who developed into the greatest goalkeeper in Liverpool's history?

The Lincolnshire town proved to be a happy hunting ground for Shanks and low budget shopping as he paid the Iron £33,000 for future two-time European Footballer of the Year, Kevin Keegan.

However, it wasn't just Shanks who had an eye for a bargain as Bob Paisley proved

DON'T ALWAYS HAVE TO BREAK THE BANK TO LAND TOP QUALITY TALENT

with his acquisition of legendary full-back Phil Neal in 1974.

The Northampton Town youngster was signed for just £66,000 and went on to collect more winners medals than any player in Liverpool's history.

Such inspired signings are more difficult to come across in today's transfer market, where a worldwide network of scouts and youth set-ups are in place to stop the next 'big thing' from slipping through the system.

But that doesn't mean it cannot happen, a fact Gerard Houllier proved with three signings that played a significant role in the cup treble of 2001.

Markus Babbel was widely regarded as one of the best defenders in Europe when it was announced he would be signing for Liverpool on a Bosman free transfer.

The fact his Reds career came to an abrupt end due to the effects of Guillain Barre Syndrome does not detract from his immense influence throughout that campaign.

Gary McAllister was perhaps the surprise signing of the summer of 2000.

His arrival was met with derision in some quarters as people wondered why a club the size of Liverpool was signing a player in his mid-30s, but his impact as a free transfer signing during his two years at Anfield was such that he is now regarded as a Liverpool legend.

But when it comes to the Reds' best value for money signing of recent times you only have to look as far as Sami Hyypia.

The giant Finn has excelled during his eight years with the Reds and in his prime he was regarded as one of the best defenders in the world.

At a cost of just £2.5million he has proved to be a rare transfer coup in the business world that is now football – especially when you consider Manchester United paid £30 million for Rio Ferdinand.

SPLASHING THE CASH

A BREAKDOWN OF HOW LIVERPOOL MANAGERS HAVE SPENT THEIR SUMMER TRANSFER FUNDS OVER THE LAST 10 YEARS

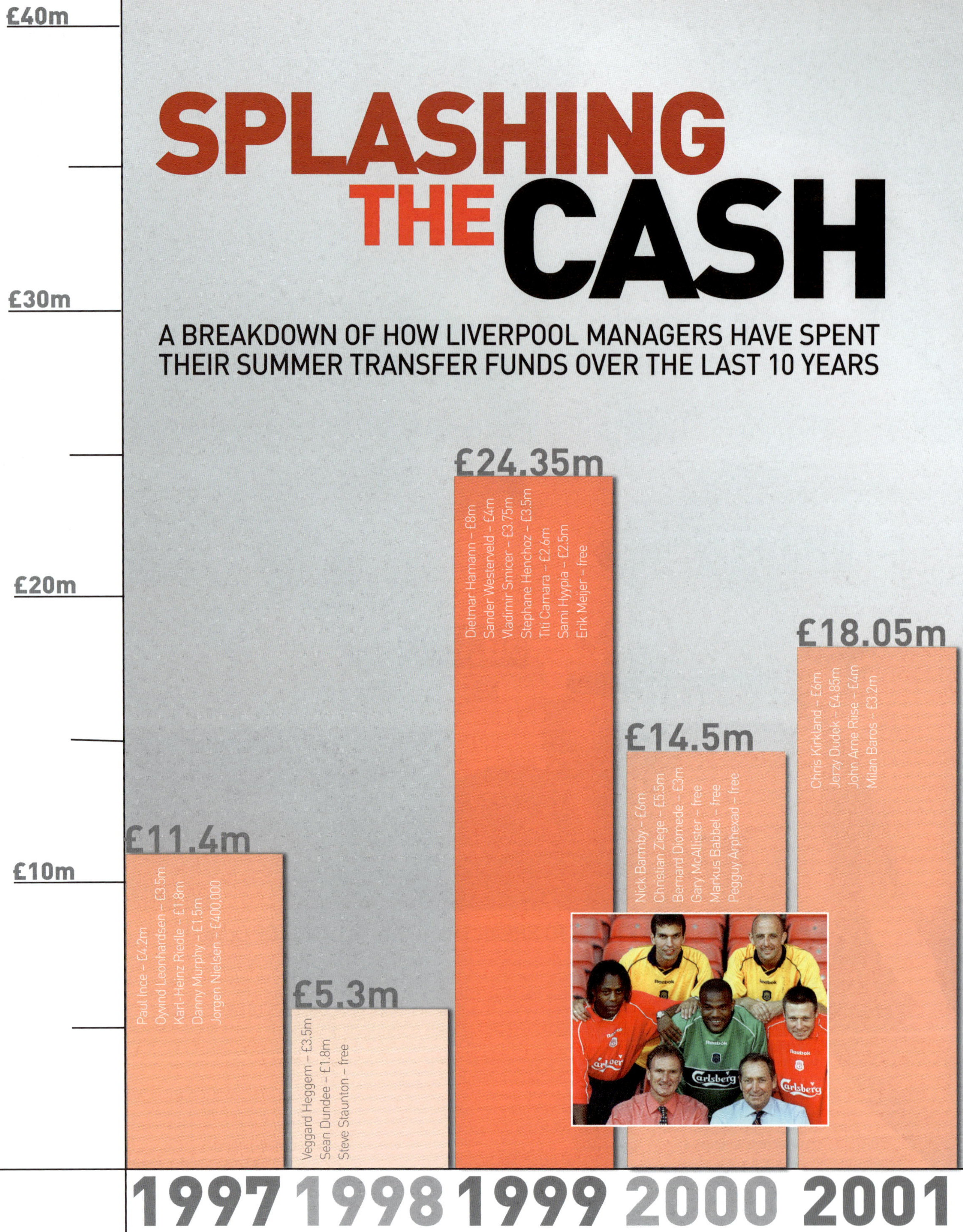

The day I signed . . .

"It was midnight on a summer's night in 1981. There was no game, but it was the night I signed for Liverpool and I went out on the pitch just to soak up the surroundings. It was incredible, every player's dream come true. That was what changed my career, a turning point in my life and I will never forget it."

MARK LAWRENSON

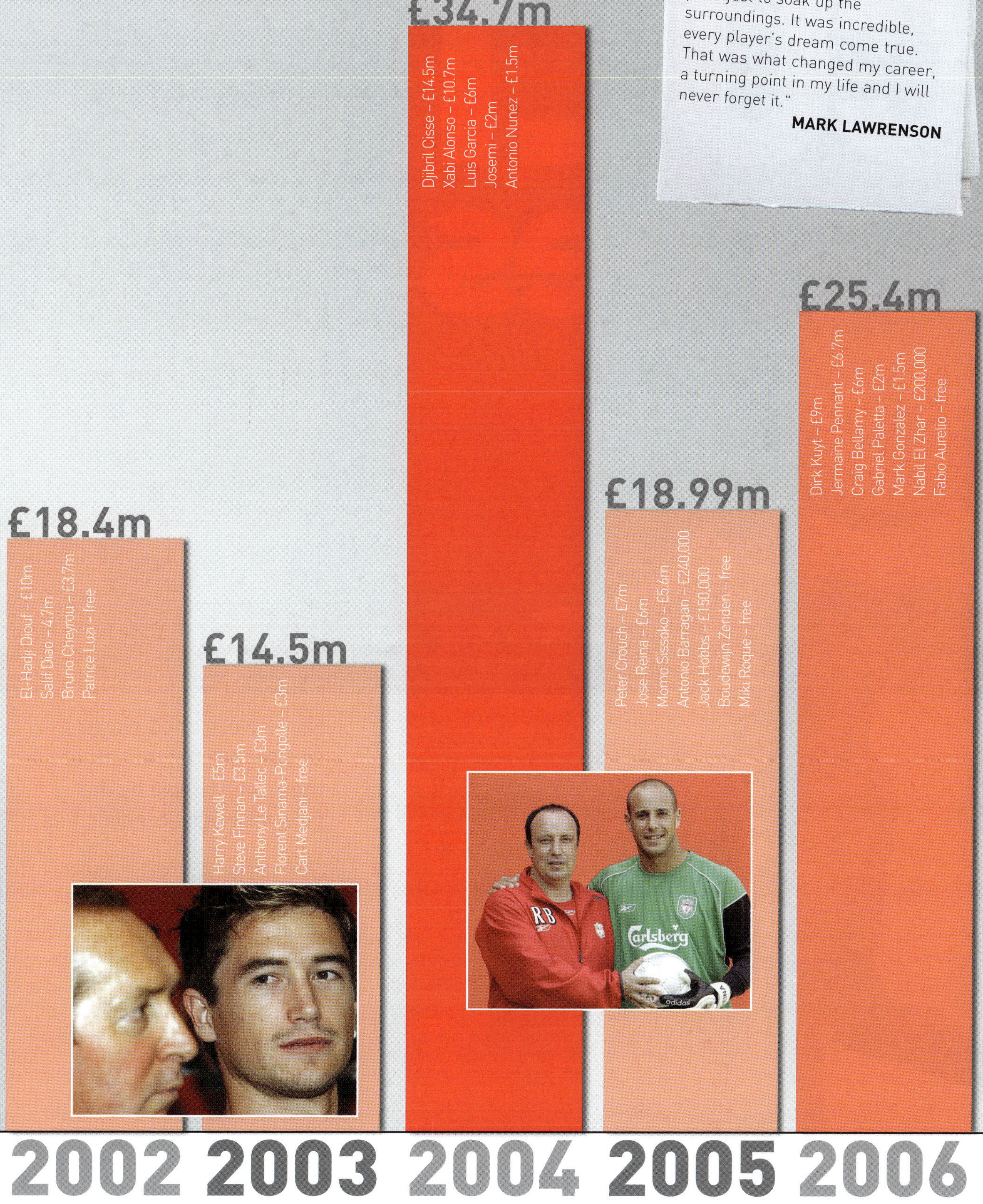

CULT heroes

PROFESSIONALISM, fitness and dedication are all qualities needed by a player to be a success on the football field in the modern era.

They are characteristics inherent in teams that win trophies and are what both clubs and fans expect from their players.

Indeed the days of George Best, Charlie Nicholas and Paul Gascoigne – men who subscribed to the play hard and party hard lifestyle – are a thing of the past.

But while fans want to see their idols in tip-top condition, they have inevitably been starved of the type of character that was a prominent figure in a generation that seems to have had its day.

The sight of a lovable rogue who enjoyed cult status with the fans, bantering with the crowd wherever possible, is something that has been less evident in the game as it has continued its evolution into a global business.

Players are treated like machines and with so much at stake there is less room for the type of character that attains cult status.

Kenny Dalglish, Ian Rush and Steven Gerrard are just some of the names that roll off the tongue when you think of Liverpool legends, but those that are privy to cult status are less celebrated names and are few and far between.

Some were good players, some were not, but all of them were loved by the fans for their eccentricities

They may well have been less talented than some of our greatest players but the likes of Joey Jones, Erik Meijer, Bruce Grobbelaar and Igor Biscan have earned a place in the supporters' hearts for different reasons.

Joey subscribed to the old adage that 'football is a man's game.'

No nonsense tackling combined with passion and unparalleled commitment marked him out as an instant Kop hero.

What he lacked in ability he made up for in enthusiasm and his colourful character inspired the famous European Cup final

Fans' favourites: Bruce Grobbelaar dresses as the Joker, while Joey Jones (below), Erik Meijer (above) and Igor Biscan (far left) were cult figures at Anfield

banner in 1977 that read: "Joey ate the frogs legs, made the Swiss roll, now he's munching Gladbach."

Brucie was another player with an added 'quality' to his personality. His antics saw him christened the 'clown prince' and his reputation for arguing and joking with the crowd as well as having a scrap or two with his team-mates turned him into a crowd favourite.

His whacky character saw people take a liking to him and his experience fighting in the jungles of Africa stood him out from your everyday footballer.

Many felt he did not have the ability to follow in the footsteps of Ray Clemence but for all his showmanship he was actually a very talented goalkeeper and his famous wobbly legs routine in Rome in 1984 set up Liverpool's fourth European Cup win.

While Brucie enjoyed a long and successful career with the Reds, featuring in over 600 matches, other cult heroes were more famed for their lack of action.

One such example is Erik Meijer, a striker who played just 27 times for Liverpool.

The Dutchman signed for the Reds on a free transfer in 1999 and, although his performances on the pitch were less than memorable, it was his personality that

caught the Kop's imagination.

From selling his house to Jari Litmanen for a profit through to naming recipes after his team-mates and putting them on his personal website, he was something a bit different from your run-of-the-mill footballer.

Another Houllier signing who became a cult icon was Igor Biscan – a squad player that didn't quite match the reputation he had forged ahead of his big money move to Anfield in December 2000.

The Croatian midfielder always seemed to have an air of bewilderment about him and it wasn't until Rafa Benitez took him under his wing that he showed any kind of form.

In the injury ravaged run to the 2005 Champions League final the quirky midfielder enjoyed his finest hour, starring with a Zinedine Zidane-type performance in the 1-0 away win over Deportivo La Coruna.

He also scored probably his best Liverpool goal in a 4-2 win at Fulham when he sheepishly celebrated a 25-yard thunderbolt.

His rise from mediocrity inspired chants of "Igor, Igor" from the Kop and the cameo moments of dribbling genius – where he probably didn't know what was going on himself – mark him down among the privileged few who have become the club's cult legends.

He did it the MEIJER WAY

FORMER ANFIELD CULT HERO ERIK MEIJER WAS A LIMITED PLAYER, BUT WAS LOVED BY REDS FANS. BUT WHAT MADE HIM SO POPULAR?

WHEN it comes to Liverpool legends Erik Meijer doesn't really come close.

In less than two seasons at the club he scored just two goals, both of which came against the might of Hull City in the League Cup.

But when you are talking about players who enjoyed a cult status at Anfield, men who have in some way endeared themselves to the Kop, 'Mad Erik' is up there with the best of them.

Brought in on a free transfer from Bayer Leverkusen in the summer of 1999, Meijer was the targetman Gerard Houllier hoped would complement the diminutive strike force of Robbie Fowler and Michael Owen.

It didn't quite work out that way but when he was given his opportunity in the first team his never-say-die attitude and tireless work ethic at the very least, earned him the respect of the fans in the stands.

But what was it that saw him take his place as one of Liverpool's greatest cult icons?

It certainly wasn't his goalscoring record that's for sure.

No, the reason Meijer is still remembered with affection by so many Reds fans to this day is – to put it politely – because of his slightly unhinged character.

Indeed, the famous ditty doing the rounds at the time summed him up in a

OWEN
10

Reebok

way only the Liverpool crowd can: "He's mad, he's red, he's off his f*****g head, Erik Meijer, Erik Meijer."

A legendary moment was recounted in the August 2003 edition of 'The Kop' magazine when Meijer was playing for a Liverpool reserves side winning 4-0 with less than a minute of the match remaining.

The story goes like this...

"Meijer chased down one full-back who passed the ball to his keeper. Meijer chased the keeper down, who gave it to his other full-back. Meijer chased the other full-back down and launched into a challenge that took the ball out for a throw-in.

"He promptly jumped to his feet and shook his fist towards a crowd of about six men and a dog as if he'd just scored the winning goal in a cup final. That was Mad Erik for you. Once he had that red shirt on he would do anything for Liverpool."

Such tales are what create the persona of the cult hero and proves that even in today's world where football is a business, there is still a place for loveable characters – regardless of their limitations.

Meijer may only have made 27 appearances for the Reds but it is certainly a time he looks back on fondly and he openly admits that the club still has a very special place in his heart.

In fact, he is still a fervent supporter of the Reds, having followed them since his childhood, and he even claims that his favourite memory associated with Liverpool was as a fan and not as a player.

"The first thing I do each week is check on Liverpool's results to see who has scored and see how they have played," he once told LFC magazine.

"On Monday evenings over here (in Germany – Meijer was playing for Hamburg at the time) they show the most important matches from the English, Italian and Spanish leagues so I am always getting information.

"I will never forget the day of the UEFA Cup final in Dortmund.

"I was in the square before the match. Apart from my wedding I haven't had such a good time!

"I was with a couple of mates. They were wearing shirts with Meijer on the back. I was wearing a Liverpool shirt but I had a jacket over it.

"As soon as the fans saw me on that square, I had to sing songs with them. It was an unbelievable atmosphere.

"The game itself was the most amazing one I have seen. In fact, it was the most perfect day all round."

'I will never forget the day of the UEFA Cup final in Dortmund. I was in the square before the match. Apart from my wedding I haven't had such a good time!'

The day I signed . . .

"When I signed for Liverpool Shanks told me Tommy Lawrence was past his best and if I continued to improve I'd be in the "big team", as he used to call it, within six months. When I got to Liverpool for pre-season after signing for them I found out that Tommy was at the peak of his career and I had to wait 2½ years before getting a regular first team place."

RAY CLEMENCE

"Shanks said to me: 'I´ve got two pieces of advice for you - don't overeat in that hotel and don't lose your accent."

KENNY DALGLISH reveals what the great Bill Shankly said on the day he signed for Bob Paisley's Liverpool

In with the fans: Erik Meijer joined the Liverpool supporters in Dortmund before the UEFA Cup final with Alaves

Hits & misses

Signed by Roy Evans

THREE OF THE BEST, THREE OF THE WORST

FOLLOWING the disappointment of Graeme Souness' spell as manager, the Reds turned to the old school to try and restore the club's flagging reputation.

The man charged with the task was bootroom legend Roy Evans, a former player who had joined the club in 1965 and been there ever since.

After taking over midway through the 1993/94 season he knew he had a big job on his hands and went about stamping his own mark on the team.

Armed with a substantial war chest he spent heavily on defensive reinforcements during the close season, having seen the Reds ship 55 Premier League goals a year earlier.

First in were John Scales and Phil Babb from Wimbledon and Coventry City respectively.

The centre-backs arrived for two massive fees but in a promising debut season they both did their bit as part of a three-man defence that saw the Reds improve their defensive record, conceding 37 goals in the league.

Evans had achieved his first target of making Liverpool more difficult to beat and he had also turned them into one of the most attractive sides to watch in the country.

When he splashed the cash once again in the summer of 1995 to bring both Stan Collymore and Jason McAteer to the club, the Reds appeared to be on the verge of greatness.

But the success never transpired and although he brought Patrik Berger to the club the quality of his signings began to diminish with the likes of Bjorn Tore Kvarme, Oyvind Leonhardsen, Paul Ince, Karl-Heinz Riedle and Brad Friedel all failing to live up to their reputations.

If there was a criticism to make on Evans' transfer policy it was perhaps his reluctance to bring in an experienced number two to compete with David James – an oversight that ultimately hindered the club's title bid in 1996/97.

It was as close as he came to adding to the League Cup success of 1995 and by the time Gerard Houllier arrived as joint manager in 1998 the writing was on the wall for Evans and he left the club within four months.

*** Roy Evans spent £43.1million on 21 players and sold 22players for £15.45million**

Reebok
Reebok

VEGGARD HEGGEM

A TALENTED right-back who was forced to cut short his career at the age of just 27, Veggard Heggem rose to prominence when he scored a famous winner when Rosenborg beat AC Milan in the San Siro.

Having converted from a right winger into a full-back his adventurous runs to the byline attracted the attention of some of Europe's top clubs and when Roy Evans and Gerard Houllier paid £3.5million for his services, he continued to impress.

But like Rob Jones before him, injuries were to take their toll, and despite some impressive displays including tremendous solo efforts in 3-1 wins over Middlesbrough and Bradford City in 1998 and 1999 respectively, he could never quite stay fit and although he began to come back in the 2000/01 season, another injury effectively ended his Reds career.

HITS

PATRIK BERGER

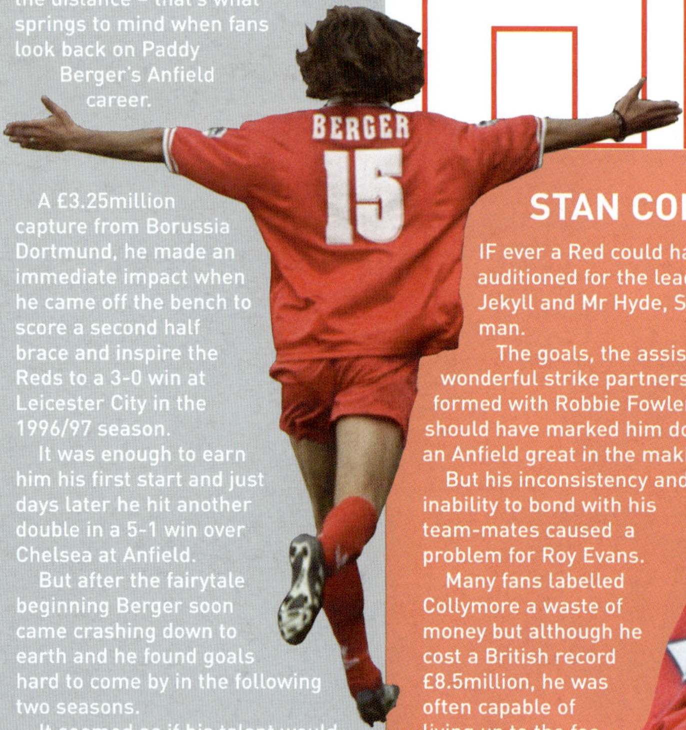

FLAIR, invention but most of all an eagerness to shoot regardless of the distance – that's what springs to mind when fans look back on Paddy Berger's Anfield career.

A £3.25million capture from Borussia Dortmund, he made an immediate impact when he came off the bench to score a second half brace and inspire the Reds to a 3-0 win at Leicester City in the 1996/97 season.

It was enough to earn him his first start and just days later he hit another double in a 5-1 win over Chelsea at Anfield.

But after the fairytale beginning Berger soon came crashing down to earth and he found goals hard to come by in the following two seasons.

It seemed as if his talent would never be fully realised at Anfield but just as it seemed he would move on to pastures new, the arrival of Gerard Houllier revitalised his Reds career.

Playing on the left side of midfield he was a big part of the 2001 treble season.

A fans' favourite for his ability to score spectacular goals, Berger's undoubted quality marks him out as a one of Evans' best value for money signings.

STAN COLLYMORE

IF ever a Red could have auditioned for the lead role in Dr Jekyll and Mr Hyde, Stan was the man.

The goals, the assists and the wonderful strike partnership he formed with Robbie Fowler should have marked him down as an Anfield great in the making.

But his inconsistency and inability to bond with his team-mates caused a problem for Roy Evans.

Many fans labelled Collymore a waste of money but although he cost a British record £8.5million, he was often capable of living up to the fee.

The partnership with Fowler produced 102 goals in just two seasons and he can claim to have played a major role in re-establishing Liverpool as a top side.

One of the highlights during his time at Anfield was the winner in the dramatic 4-3 win over Newcastle but his bad boy reputation took its toll and he was finally sold on to Aston Villa.

SEAN DUNDEE

ONE of the most disappointing signings in the history of the club, Sean 'Crocodile' Dundee arrived at Anfield with a decent reputation for scoring goals in the Bundesliga.

In fact, the German national team had made overtures towards the possibility of him becoming a German citizen and playing for 'Die Nationalelf.'

However, any hopes that we had signed the Gerd Muller of his generation were well and truly crushed once we saw him in action.

A lumbering forward who somehow convinced Roy Evans that he was a professional footballer, he made just five appearances for the Reds, never starting a game and never scoring a goal.

MICHAEL STENSGAARD

MICHAEL STENSGAARD is a former Denmark U21 international goalkeeper who is remembered more for his mishap while ironing rather than his playing career at Liverpool.

Signed from Hvidovre for £400,000 in May 1994, Stensgaard was hailed as one of the finest young keepers in Europe.

But despite his potential he did not manage to play one first team match for Liverpool and after just three seasons with the club was forced to retire from the game when he injured his shoulder while taking the ironing board out at home.

It is not the best way to be remembered and when you consider that he was being tipped to become a future Liverpool and Denmark number one, it was not only a waste of money, but a waste of talent.

MISSES

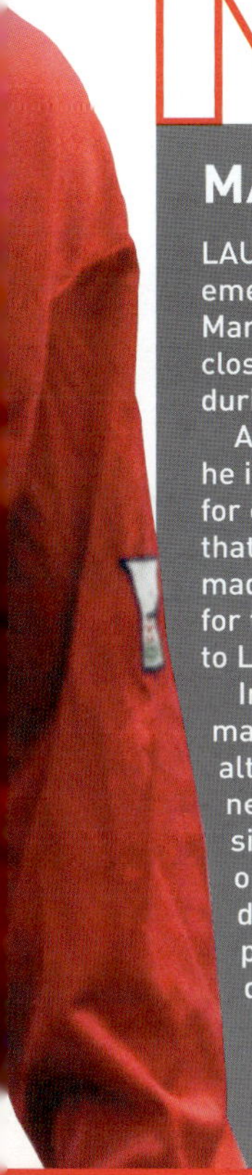

MARK KENNEDY

LAUDED as one of the finest emerging talents in British football, Mark Kennedy never once came close to living up to his billing during his three years at Anfield.

A £2million signing from Millwall he is best remembered at Anfield for off the field problems and a shot that struck the crossbar when he made his debut as a late substitute for the Reds in a 1-0 defeat at home to Leeds United in 1995.

In four seasons at Liverpool he made just 21 appearances and although many fans felt he was never given a decent run in the side, when he was given an opportunity his lack of determination led to him being pushed out of the Melwood exit door.

Hits & misses

Signed by Graeme Souness

THREE OF THE BEST, THREE OF THE WORST

WHEN Graeme Souness replaced Kenny Dalglish as Liverpool manager he decided a complete squad overhaul was needed if he was to return the Reds to the summit of English football.

It was a drastic decision and one that ultimately ended in disaster with a series of expensive flops seeing Liverpool plummet from regular title challengers into a club scrapping for a top six place.

The likes of Peter Beardsley, Steve Staunton and Steve McMahon were deemed past their best by the former Rangers boss and while they went on to prove they still had an abundance of quality to offer, their replacements could not reach the level required to play for a club of Liverpool's calibre.

Souness' signings read like a 'who's who' of flops with Paul Stewart, Julian Dicks, Torben Piechnik and Nigel Clough leading the way as top earners who failed to live up to their price tags.

Unfortunately for Souey his impact as boss did not match the success of his playing days and he will be remembered as the man that ended Liverpool's period of success that spanned the 70s and 80s.

Although he does deserve some credit for bringing the likes of Rob Jones and Stig Inge Bjornebye to the club, his overall record in the transfer market was little more than shocking.

*** Souness bought 15 players for £17.94million and sold 21 players for £9.825million.**

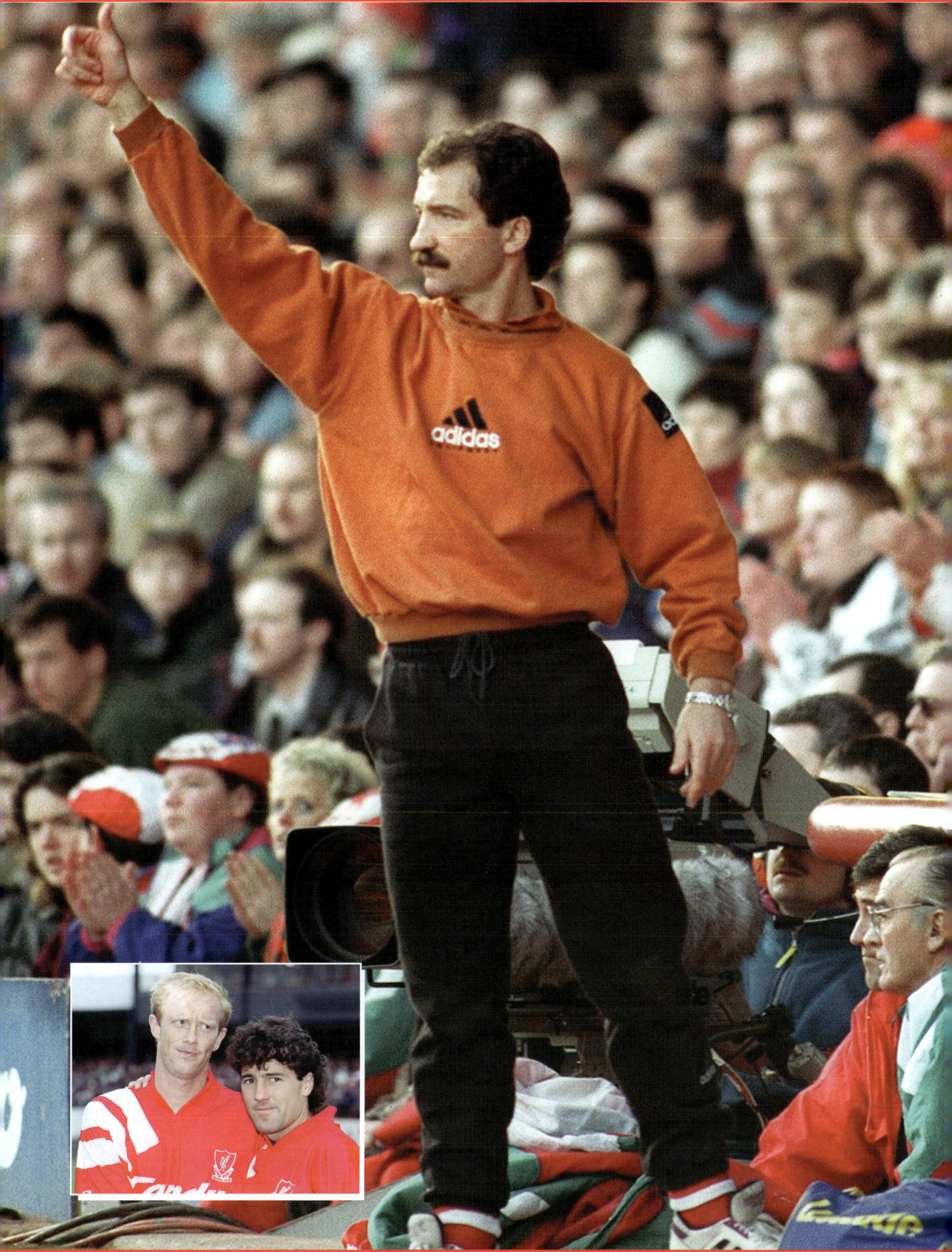
adidas

MARK WRIGHT

A STAR of England's heroic fourth place finish at Italia '90, Wright was identified by Graeme Souness as the man who could restore solidity to Liverpool's defence.

The £2.2 million fee paid to Derby County in the summer of 1991 was a British record for a defender and it was therefore important for both Wright and Souness, that the player made a strong start.

However, after just two matches he was sidelined with injury and when he did return after three months out he failed to recapture his best form.

In the absence of Ronnie Whelan he was named captain and he ended the season on a high when he lifted the FA Cup after a 2-0 win over Sunderland.

He was dropped for the majority of Liverpool's matches the following campaign and his attitude was questioned by new boss Roy Evans a year later.

But at the start of the 1995/96 season he returned to pre-season determined to prove people wrong and enjoyed two magnificent seasons before announcing his retirement in 1998 having restored his reputation.

HITS

STIG INGE BJORNEBYE

A NORWEGIAN international signed from Rosenborg, Bjornebye arrived at Liverpool having just scored the winning goal in the Norwegian Cup final.

It was a dream period in his life that soon turned into a nightmare as he made his Reds debut in a 5-1 thrashing at Coventry City, a defeat that was Liverpool's biggest loss in 16 years.

Playing at left-back he struggled to cope with the standard of the Premier League and did not make much of an impact in his first two seasons with the club.

But when Roy Evans opted for a five man defensive formation Stig was moved into a left-wing back role and began to forge a reputation as one of the finest crossers of the ball in England.

His finest period in a Reds shirt came in the 1996/97 season when he was named in the Premier League team of the year and he proved that the £600,000 Souness paid for him was money well spent.

ROB JONES

FOR all the big money signings brought in by Graeme Souness, the £300,000 fee he paid for unknown full-back Rob Jones proved to be his most astute piece of business as Reds boss.

Signed from Crewe Alexandra in 1991, Jones made an instant impact when he marked the media darling of the time – Ryan Giggs – out of a 0-0 draw with Manchester United at Old Trafford, just 48 hours after appearing in a fourth division match with the Railwaymen.

His marauding runs down the right flank and later as a right wing-back in Roy Evans' attacking side of the mid-90s, made him a Kop favourite during his time at Anfield and it was a travesty that he did not go on to win a hatful of caps for England.

But Jones, or 'Trigger' as he was known by his team-mates, was constantly troubled by back and knee injuries and won just eight caps for his country.

The continuous wear and tear on his body began to take its toll and he finally left Liverpool in May 1999, having famously failed to find the net in 243 matches for the Reds.

He attempted to resurrect his career at West Ham, but after playing less than two matches he was forced to hang up his boots at the age of 27.

TORBEN PIECHNIK

"IT'S no Piechnik for Torben."

One of the finest newspaper headlines of recent times and yet the nightmare endured by Torben Piechnik on his Liverpool debut was to sum up his brief time with the club.

Despite starring for Denmark in their surprise Euro '92 success, Piechnik never looked the part in a Reds shirt and although Souness initially stuck by his £500,000 capture from FC Copenhagen, he was eventually dropped during the run-in to the 1992/93 season.

By the start of the next campaign his Liverpool career was well and truly on the wane and when he was drafted in to an injury-hit side for the trip to Newcastle his performance was so poor that he was hauled off at half-time.

Unsurprisingly he never played for Souness or Liverpool again.

MISSES

ISTVAN KOZMA

THE signing of Istvan Kozma perhaps offered an insight into the lack of quality on show in the Scottish Premier League.

A £300,000 capture from Dunfermline, the Hungarian international was a player Souness had taken a liking to during his successful spell as Rangers boss.

However, Kozma was never going to match the likes of Billy Liddell and John Barnes in terms of wing wizardry and his appearances on the flank were restricted to just three starts and 10 appearances in total.

His one moment of glory for Liverpool came in a 4-4 draw with Chesterfield in the League Cup.

His appearance as a substitute saw him create two goals and help the Reds rescue a replay after the Reds had trailed 3-0 at one stage.

PAUL STEWART

HOW do you fill the void in midfield left by a legend like Steve McMahon?

Whatever the answer may have been it certainly wasn't 'buy Paul Stewart'.

Graeme Souness made some poor signings during his spell as Reds boss, but of all the big money flops who arrived at Melwood, few could argue that Stewart proved to be one of the most disappointing.

The former Tottenham midfielder cost the Reds a fortune in the summer of 1992 when they shelled out £2.3million for his services.

42 appearances in four years was a poor return for that money.

And yet it had all begun in positive fashion when he scored a winner in a 2-1 victory over Sheffield United on his Anfield debut.

It didn't get much better than that though and despite being surplus to requirements he did not appear interested in leaving.

He remained at Liverpool until the summer of 1996, going out on loan several times until his contract ran out.

Hits & misses

Signed by Kenny Dalglish

THREE OF THE BEST, THREE OF THE WORST

KING' Kenny Dalglish undoubtedly had the Midas touch during his time as a player at Anfield, but when he started to show the same winning qualities in the dugout the Reds knew they were on to a winner.

The famous number seven became the club's first and only player manager and enjoyed a sensational debut season in 1985/86 when the Reds overcame a troubled start to claim the league and FA Cup double.

It was a tremendous achievement given that the club had suffered the trauma of the Heysel Stadium disaster just 12 months earlier.

However, the following season saw the club finish empty handed and with Ian Rush saying 'arrivederci' and heading to Italy, Kenny was faced with his first major test in the transfer market.

It was one he passed with flying colours as he used the money from Rush's sale to bring in some of English football's brightest talents.

John Barnes and Peter Beardsley were already two of England's best international footballers when they turned up at Melwood and with Kenny having already added John Aldridge and Nigel Spackman to his side, the Reds were all set to win back their title.

They did this with aplomb, playing some of the finest football Anfield has ever seen and proving that Kenny had evolved from world class player into one of the game's most astute managers.

Looking back at Dalglish's record in the transfer market it is obvious that he had a good eye for an attacking player and the likes of Ray Houghton, Steve McMahon and Steve Staunton can also claim to be on his list of successes.

But as the pressure began to mount post-Hillsborough, it is perhaps significant that the calibre of his signings began to diminish.

The likes of Glenn Hysen, Jimmy Carter and David Speedie all failed to inspire, although one of Kenny's last acts in the transfer market saw him bring in future club captain Jamie Redknapp from Bournemouth.

*** Kenny Dalglish bought 23 players for £12.535million and sold 20 players for £6.767million**

STEVE McMAHON

STEVE McMAHON was Kenny Dalglish's first signing as Reds boss and proved to be one of his most influential.

A midfield hardman in the Graeme Souness mould, McMahon's leadership qualities and all-action midfield style made him an instant hit at Anfield.

The fact the boyhood Blue had seen the error of his ways and opted to move across Stanley Park via a two-year spell with Aston Villa earned him a few brownie points with Kopites too.

In seven seasons at Anfield he played 277 matches and became a symbolic figure of the Dalglish era, combining hard work and a desire to win with an assured touch of class.

HITS

JOHN ALDRIDGE

REPLACING one moustacheoed goal machine with another is no mean feat, but that's exactly what Liverpool did when they paid £750,000 to Oxford United to bring in the free-scoring John Aldridge.

The scouse hit-man was brought in to succeed Ian Rush, and once he was given a run in the side he made such a huge impact that reports at the time suggested Juventus thought they had been sold the wrong player!

With John Barnes and Peter Beardsley providing the ammunition, Aldo excelled and hit an astonishing 45 goals to help the Reds towards title number 17.

But when King Kenny brought Rushie back just one year later, it spelled the end for Aldridge, despite the fact he netted 47 league goals in his two full seasons with the Reds.

With Dalglish's preference for a Rush-Beardsley partnership, the Ireland international did not want to spend half his time on the bench and opted for a change when he moved to Real Sociedad in 1989.

He may have only played 104 games for Liverpool, but Kopites still recall fondly the fairytale moment he came off the bench to score a penalty at the Kop end in his final match for the Reds.

JOHN BARNES

"BARNES did what we expected him to do. He made a goal, scored one, and entertained. You remember that."

Those were the words of Kenny Dalglish after seeing John Barnes turn on the style on his Anfield debut at home to Oxford United in September 1987.

It is a quote that could have been uttered after any number of the 407 matches he played for Liverpool.

The £900,000 fee paid to Watford for the left winger's services was a large sum at the time, but he was more than worth the outlay as 'Digger' went on to establish himself as one of the finest Reds players of all time.

His skill, vision and finishing ability made him the stand-out player in Kenny Dalglish's team of entertainers and saw him net the player of the year awards in 1987/88 and 1989/90.

Although his ability to mesmerise and beat defenders at will faded as a result of continued problems with his hamstring, he managed to re-invent himself as a cultured central midfielder and went on to enjoy what was a glorious 10-year spell at Anfield before leaving for Newcastle United on a free transfer in August 1997.

He was a Liverpool legend and one of Dalglish's best pieces of business.

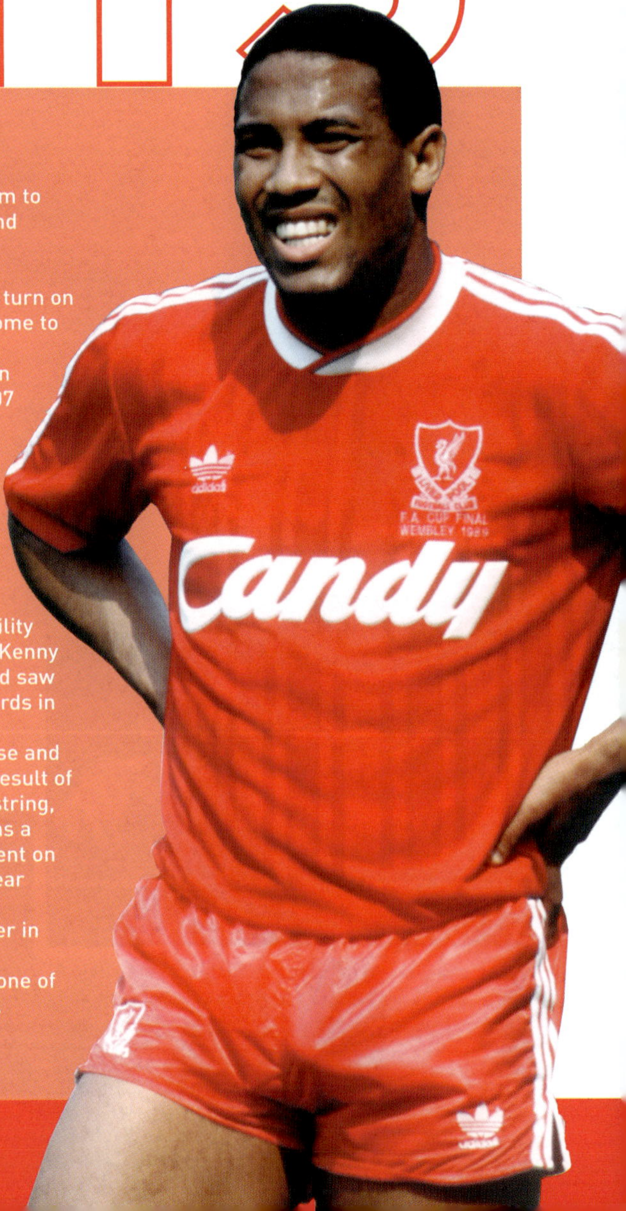

NICKY TANNER

A PLAYER of limited ability, Nick Tanner was a young defender who never truly made the grade during his five seasons at Liverpool.

Signed from the lower leagues for £20,000 he didn't look capable of stepping up to the first team and rarely started under Dalglish.

At the time of his surprise move to Anfield he was on the verge of signing for Torquay United and that says it all really.

Needless to say he shocked the football world and opted for Liverpool.

However, under Graeme Souness he somehow became a fixture of the Liverpool defence and we became accustomed to an uncomfortable looking Tanner hoofing the ball upfield.

Sadly his Liverpool dream ended in 1994 when he was forced into early retirement with persistent back trouble.

MISSES

JIMMY CARTER

ONE of the poorest players to have ever donned the liver bird upon his chest, Jimmy Carter was probably 'King' Kenny's worst signing as Liverpool boss.

Such was his impact at Anfield that Arsenal must have been laughing all the way to the bank when Kenny paid £800,000 for the woeful winger.

In two seasons at the club he made just eight appearances and looked totally out of his depth.

Question marks were raised when it first emerged the club had signed him and it was his arrival that perhaps highlights just how much the stress was affecting Dalglish's judgement at the time.

ALAN IRVINE

ALAN who?

The younger generation of Reds can be forgiven for asking the question.

Signed in October 1986 Scottish-born Irvine failed to make any impact during his time at Liverpool, making just four appearances and failing to earn a single start.

Impressively, however, those four appearances took in the three different domestic competitions as he played twice in the league, once in the League Cup and once in the FA Cup.

With a host of top forwards way ahead of him in the pecking order, he was rarely given a chance and moved on less than a year after Dalglish paid Falkirk £75,000 for his services.

SEASON 2007/08 FIXTURES

August

SET	11	Aston Villa (A) 5.15pm
	14/15	CL 3rd qualifier 1st leg
SKY	**19**	**Chelsea (H) 4.00pm**
SKY	25	Sunderland (A) 12.45pm
	28/29	CL 3rd qualifier 2nd leg

September

	01	**Derby County (H)**
SKY	15	Portsmouth (A) 12.45pm
	18/19	CL Group match 1
	22	**Birmingham City (H)**
	25/26	Carling Cup 3rd round
	29	Wigan Athletic (A)

October

	02/03	CL Group match 2
	07	**Tottenham Hotspur (H)**
SKY	20	Everton (A) 12.45pm
	23/24	CL Group match 3
SKY	**28**	**Arsenal (H) 4.00pm**
	30/31	Carling Cup 4th round

November

SET	03	Blackburn Rovers (A) 5.15pm
	06/07	CL Group match 4
SET	**10**	**Fulham (H) 5.15pm**
SKY	24	Newcastle Utd (A) 12.45pm
	27/28	CL Group match 5

December

01	**Bolton Wanderers (H)**
04/05	Carling Cup 5th round
08	Reading (A)
11/12	CL Group match 6
15	**Man United (H)**
22	**Portsmouth (H)**
26	Derby County (A)
29	Man City (A)

January

01	**Wigan Athletic (H)**
05/06	FA Cup 3rd round
08/09	Carling Cup Semi-final 1st leg
12	Middlesbrough (A)
19	**Aston Villa (H)**
22/23	Carling Cup Semi-final 2nd leg
26/27	FA Cup 4th round
29	West Ham United (A)

February

02	**Sunderland (H)**
09	Chelsea (A)
16/17	FA Cup 5th round
19/20	CL last 16 1st leg
23	**Middlesbrough (H)**
24	Carling Cup Final (Wembley)

March

01	Bolton Wanderers (A)
04/05	CL last 16 2nd leg
08	**Newcastle United (H)**
08/09	FA Cup 6th round
15	**Reading (H)**
22	Man United (A)
29	**Everton (H)**

April

01/02	CL quarter-final 1st leg
04	Arsenal (A)
05/06	FA Cup semi-final
08/09	CL quarter-final 2nd leg
12	**Blackburn Rovers (H)**
19	Fulham (A)
22/23	CL semi-final 1st leg
25	Birmingham City (A)
29/30	CL semi-final 1st leg

May

03	**Man City (H)**
10	Tottenham Hotspur (A)
17	FA Cup Final (Wembley)
21	CL Final (Moscow)
TBC	**West Ham United (H)**

All dates subject to further change by TV companies. UEFA Champions League dates are provisional.

SKY Live on Sky Sports
SET Live on Setanta

Hits & misses

Signed by Joe Fagan

THREE OF THE BEST, THREE OF THE WORST

A QUIET, unassuming man, Joe Fagan's brief tenure as Reds boss was mixed with success and tragedy.

Having taken over the reigns from the departing Bob Paisley he led Liverpool to a league, European Cup and Milk Cup treble in 1984 before bowing out in infamous circumstances after the Heysel Stadium tragedy of 1985.

Who can forget the moment he returned to Liverpool after the final and broke down in tears? It was a sad way for him to say farewell but it did not detract from his success as manager.

His brief forays into the transfer market saw him bring in players who did not reach the heights of other additions that became icons of both the Bill Shankly and Bob Paisley eras but he can at least claim that there were few major flops.

His first signing was Gary Gillespie in 1983, a player who remained at Anfield for eight years, while the likes of Michael Robinson and Paul Walsh had their fair share of great moments in a Liverpool shirt.

Of the eight players brought in during his spell as manager only Wayne Harrison failed to make any sort of impact at Anfield and with the likes of John Wark and Jan Molby he added players with talent and goalscoring ability that would go on to excel and produce the goods under Kenny Dalglish.

*** Joe Fagan bought eight players for £2.565million and sold five players for £990,000.**

JOHN WARK

A CLASSY midfielder with an eye for goal, John Wark enjoyed a successful, but injury blighted, spell at Anfield.

A star of the famous Ipswich Town sides of the late 1970s and early 1980s, Wark was signed for £450,000 and quickly settled into life at Liverpool.

In his first full season he finished as the club's leading scorer with 27 goals to his name – including three hat-tricks – as the Reds reached the European Cup final and finished second in the league.

However, his contribution to the double winning season in 1985/86 was wrecked by injury and from then on he was used sparingly in the Liverpool midfield.

After just under five seasons at Anfield he was sold back to Ipswich having scored 42 goals in 108 games.

HITS

GARY GILLESPIE

A BALL-PLAYING centre-half who arrived with a big reputation from Coventry City, the signing of Gary Gillespie proved to be an astute piece of business by Joe Fagan.

Faced with the difficult task of displacing Alan Hansen or Mark Lawrenson at the heart of the Liverpool defence, he was initially used as a right-back.

But his presence in the side was such that it forced new player/manager Kenny Dalglish into a re-think and he moved Lawrenson to full-back in order to accommodate the Scot.

Breaking up one of the best centre-back partnerships in Liverpool's history is no mean achievement and for a spell Gillespie looked capable of going on to become one of the finest defenders in our history.

But injuries began to disrupt the number of games he played and he struggled to recapture his top form.

When Graeme Souness arrived as manager his number was up and he was sold to Celtic for £900,000.

JAN MOLBY

NOT even problems with his weight, booze or the law could stop Jan Molby from enjoying a lengthy and successful Liverpool career.

The Dane with the famous scouse accent had mesmeric ability and had a range of passing that would even leave Xabi Alonso envious. He also knew how to take a penalty, scoring a massive 42 times from the spot.

After signing for £200,000 from Ajax in 1984 he showed early glimpses of his genius and looked capable of filling the huge void left by Graeme Souness.

Unfortunately for both Liverpool and Molby his off-the-field problems stopped him from achieving this but when he did get fit he was well worth a place on the team sheet and still managed to rack up 292 matches in 11 seasons at the club.

PAUL WALSH

PAUL WALSH was a lively striker who never quite lived up to the form that saw him named the PFA's most promising player in the 1983/84 season.

Signed from Luton Town for £700,000, Walsh looked worth every penny when he made an immediate impact for the Reds by scoring within seconds of his Anfield debut against West Ham.

But it was to prove a false dawn as the majority of his Liverpool career would see him struggle to hold down a place in the first team.

With Ian Rush ahead of him in the pecking order he was a regular on the bench and made just 112 appearances in four seasons with the club.

He still managed a respectable total of 37 goals in that time but when Kenny Dalglish opted to sign Peter Beardsley and John Aldridge in 1987 his chances of a first team place became even more limited at Anfield and he moved to Tottenham Hotspur for £500,000.

MISSES

KEVIN MacDONALD

THE former Leicester City captain was one of the men touted as a possible replacement for Graeme Souness when he joined the Reds for £400,000 in November 1984.

It was a billing he would fail to live up to and despite featuring prominently in the 1985/86 double winning campaign, injury would effectively end his hopes of establishing himself as a regular.

After taking to the field as a substitute in a 2-1 defeat at Southampton in September 1986 he suffered a broken leg that ruled him out for over a year and when he returned he was unable to reclaim a place in the side.

WAYNE HARRISON

EARMARKED as one for the future, Wayne Harrison arrived from Oldham Athletic with an impressive reputation at youth level.

But sadly the 17-year-old failed to live up to his early promise and never came close to justifying his £250,000 fee.

Like so many youngsters who look set for stardom at a young age he failed to progress and eventually left Liverpool unnoticed having made no impression on the first team.

Hits & misses

Signed by Bob Paisley

THREE OF THE BEST, THREE OF THE WORST

IT is a well-known fact in Liverpool Football Club circles that Bob Paisley could spot a star-in-the-making very early.

He would watch a player and immediately assess in great detail his strengths and weaknesses and, most importantly, whether he was the right man for Liverpool.

While the legendary Bill Shankly is credited with laying the foundations for turning the Reds into England's most successful side, it was Paisley who won the most silverware.

And despite what some former players and observers might suggest, he did it over a sustained period of time and with his own group of players.

Paisley was known for his mild manner but he could be ruthless when it mattered and his ability to sign players that slotted effortlessly into his well-oiled Reds side saw Liverpool maintain their place as England and Europe's team to beat during his trophy-laden nine years as boss.

The list of names brought in under his stewardship reads like a 'who's who' of Liverpool legends.

Phil Neal, Terry McDermott, Alan Hansen, Kenny Dalglish, Graeme Souness, Alan Kennedy, Ronnie Whelan and Ian Rush are the pick of his signings and are proof of his magnificent record in the transfer market.

But while it may seem like Paisley could do no wrong when splashing the cash on team reinforcements, the likes of Peter McDonnell, Frank McGarvey and John McGregor went some way to proving that not even the great Bob Paisley got it right all the time.

*** Bob Paisley bought 25 players for £5.503million and sold 42 players for £3.639million.**

GRAEME SOUNESS

A LEADER of men, a born winner and the complete footballer, Graeme Souness would be one of the first names on the team sheet if you were asked to pick Liverpool's all-time greatest XI.

When he joined the Reds from Middlesbrough in 1978, the £352,000 fee was a record between two English clubs.

The fact this never came into question shows just how good Souness was.

He was a bargain and all round midfielder who could pass, tackle, shoot and head the ball – you name it Souness could do it and he could always do it better than most.

He made the club a profit when he left for Sampdoria in 1984 for £650,000, but that came after making 359 appearances for the club and his transfer went through after he'd captained the Reds to a league, European Cup and League Cup treble.

In total he won five titles, three European Cups and four League Cups during his time at the club.

He later returned to Liverpool as manager, but unlike Dalglish he could not recreate the same magic he had shown as a player.

HITS

KENNY DALGLISH

THIRTY years on from the summer that saw 'King' Kenny Dalglish sign for Liverpool he is still regarded as the finest player ever to grace the shirt.

The star man in Jock Stein's Celtic side, Dalglish was widely regarded as one of the best players in Europe when Bob Paisley brought him to Anfield.

Faced with the task of replacing the popular figure of Kevin Keegan, Dalglish not only matched the great number seven's achievements, he eclipsed them.

The fact both Paisley and Bill Shankly pointed to Kenny as Liverpool's greatest ever signing goes some way to proving his quality and every single Kopite who saw him play would unanimously agree.

IAN RUSH

IF ever a player proved that Bob Paisley had the knack of plucking players from obscurity and turning them into world class performers it was Ian Rush.

When the Welshman arrived at Liverpool from Chester City in 1980 he was a timid, awkward youngster with raw pace and a lot to learn.

But after Bob had taken him under his wing and taught him the Liverpool way, he went on to become the greatest goalscorer in the club's history.

Blessed with sizzling pace and a knack for scoring goals he formed a wonderful partnership with Kenny Dalglish and after a brief spell in Italy he returned to the club and scored another bucketful of goals before later being named captain and playing mentor to the rising star of Robbie Fowler.

The statistics illustrate what great value for money Rush was when you consider he scored 346 goals for the club and his most frequent victims were Everton, who were on the end of 25 of his goals – a Merseyside derby record.

DAVID HODGSON

BOB PAISLEY had high hopes for this England under-21 international when he paid Middlesbrough a substantial fee to bring him to Anfield.

He had hardly been prolific during his time at Ayresome Park but Paisley felt he could bring the best out of the pacy forward, just as he had done with Ian Rush.

Sadly it was never meant to be.

Despite notching four goals in his first six games, Hodgson never quite settled and when he left for Sunderland he had managed just 49 appearances in a Liverpool shirt, despite being in the Reds' squad for the 1984 European Cup final.

MISSES

AVI COHEN

A £200,000 capture from Maccabi Tel Aviv in 1979, Avi Cohen's inability to dislodge Alan Kennedy as Liverpool's left-back ultimately led to him failing to make his mark at Anfield.

The Israeli international was signed after he impressed Bob Paisley in a trial and became the first overseas player to play for Liverpool since the 1950s.

He is best remembered for his rollercoaster ride during a match with Aston Villa – a game that would see Liverpool regain the title if they won.

With the Reds leading 1-0 Cohen sliced a clearance over Ray Clemence and into the net to leave Anfield on tenterhooks.

But his nightmare soon turned into a fairytale as he made up for his error by firing the Reds ahead at the Kop end.

RICHARD MONEY

RICHARD MONEY was a highly respected England under-21 international who never lived up to his early promise.

A £50,000 buy from Fulham, he made just 17 appearances for the Reds and apart from playing his role in the famous 1-1 draw with Bayern Munich in the European Cup semi-final in 1981, he could never make a big enough impact to establish himself as a first team regular.

THE PLAYERS THAT PROVE THERE'S . . .

LIFE AFTER ANFIELD

. . . MAYBE

IT USED to be said that the only direction your career would go in once you stopped playing for Liverpool was down.

For the vast majority of players who have graced the Anfield turf and lapped up the adulation of the Kop faithful, they never experienced anything like it once they moved to pastures new.

The way the club used to operate made it likely that players would be brought in from relative obscurity, were trained in the Liverpool way, and offloaded once they were past their peak.

In the modern age of instant success, players are often at or around their peak when they are brought to the club and they either sink or swim in the pressure cooker environment of a club that expects success every year.

Not every player who has worn the famous Liver bird on their chest has enjoyed the best years of their career at Anfield however. And of those who have been successful, some have gone on to play at a high level and win trophies under different managers at different clubs.

Some, like Steve McManaman and Michael Owen, have gone on to play for another club with the highest pedigree in Europe.

Both were in their prime when they decided to leave Anfield and the fans felt betrayed when they left while they still had a lot to offer at Liverpool.

Despite being in and out of a Real Madrid team that included names like Ronaldo, Figo and Zidane, McManaman even had the pleasure of scoring a European Cup final goal after moving to Spain, although Owen's season at the Bernabeu saw him make less of an impact than he would have hoped.

Several others have left Anfield for a foreign challenge and been able to achieve abroad.

The ambitious Kevin Keegan famously went to Hamburg in 1977, leaving Reds fans wondering why he would want to leave the European champions when they were sweeping all before them domestically and on the continent.

Keegan's decision didn't turn into the dramatic downwards step people thought though as he went on to win the Bundesliga title with the Germans and reach the European Cup final in 1980.

After captaining Liverpool to a historic treble in 1984, Graeme Souness wanted to prove he could cut it abroad. It seems he could as he enjoyed his foreign success in Italy, winning the Coppa Italia with Sampdoria.

John Aldridge's spell at Anfield was all too brief for both him and the Liverpool fans, but he still enjoyed success when he left the club.

He joined Real Sociedad for £1million in September 1989 and became a huge hit with the San Sebastian crowd after scoring 40 goals in 63 games before returning to England.

Fernando Morientes was a player who enjoyed all of his success away from Liverpool. He joined the Reds from Real Madrid with a reputation as an ace goalscorer, but English football didn't agree with him and he returned to Spain to join Valencia.

Big hit: John Aldridge became a favourite with the Real Sociedad fans

It took him no time at all to re-adapt to La Liga and was one of the top scorers in Spain in 2006/07.

To show goodwill to their neighbours, Liverpool have donated several players to city rivals Everton, and some of them have made a huge impact across the park.

Johnny Morrissey and Kevin Sheedy are two examples of players who failed to make the grade at Anfield, but joined the Blues and ended up picking up medals – the latter as an intergral part of the most successful side Everton has ever had.

A more established player to have made a high profile switch to Goodison Park was Peter Beardsley. Liverpool manager Souness thought the Geordie star had seen better days, but he proved he wasn't finished at Everton and Newcastle.

While Liverpool's history is littered with examples of players who have played the best football of their careers at Anfield, El-Hadji Diouf and David James have certainly enhanced their reputations since much-publicised struggles at Liverpool.

And even though Ray Clemence is widely regarded as the best goalkeeper the club has ever had, few could deny that he was still a top class player when he moved to Spurs in 1981.

So while Liverpool may be the be-all-and-end-all to those who worship at Anfield every other week, there are a chosen few who have seen that there can sometimes be life outside of the Shankly Gates – not that many of us find that easy to believe.

Pastures new: Kevin Keegan, Peter Beardsley, Kevin Sheedy, Steve McManaman, Ray Clemence and Fernando Morientes have left Liverpool, but still had success elsewhere

Hits & misses

Signed by Bill Shankly

THREE OF THE BEST, THREE OF THE WORST

HAD Huddersfield Town shared the same vision as Bill Shankly then perhaps they would boast the honour of being the most successful side in English football history ahead of Liverpool.

Fortunately for us, they did not and when Shanks asked the Yorkshire club to finance a move for two Scottish talents by the names of Ron Yeats and Ian St John his plea fell on deaf ears.

Within months he had joined Liverpool and although the board were wary of spending so much money on two players, he convinced them it would help take the Reds to the next level.

It was a decision that would alter the club's destiny and St John and Yeats were the backbone of Shankly's revolution.

Success inevitably followed and the charismatic Scotsman went on to work wonders in the transfer market, bringing in the likes of Emlyn Hughes, Ray Clemence, John Toshack, Kevin Keegan and Jimmy Case to name but a few.

He had a happy knack of finding a player with the right attitude and mentality to prosper at Liverpool and the personality to inspire them to produce their best.

But it wasn't always a certainty that Shanks would unearth the next Anfield star and big money signings such as Alun Evans and Tony Hateley failed to make the impact he would have hoped for.

One of Shankly's most famous moves in the transfer market saw him sign young Arsenal striker Ray Kennedy for £180,000.

It was poignant for being his final act in the hot-seat as he shocked the football world by announcing his decision to retire in July 1974.

Kennedy's arrival may well have been overshadowed by Shankly's decision but he went on to become an Anfield great, proving once again that Shanks was a shrewd mover in the transfer market.

*** Shankly bought 36 players for a total of £1,329,250 and sold 50 players for £717,500.**

EMLYN HUGHES

IF ever a player was built to play for Bill Shankly it was Emlyn Hughes.

Boundless enthusiasm, remarkable energy and a thoroughbred winner, he was quite simply a leader of men.

His all-action displays and heart on the sleeve mentality made him an integral part of the team and he became a Kop favourite when he earned the nickname 'Crazy Horse' after rugby tackling Newcastle's Albert Bennet.

Captain of both Liverpool and England, he made 665 appearances for Liverpool and is the only Reds skipper to have lifted the European Cup twice.

HITS

KEVIN KEEGAN

HARD work, enthusiasm and a hunger to continuously improve saw Kevin Keegan rise to the summit of the European game.

Signed from Scunthorpe for £33,000 in 1971 the man nicknamed "Mighty Mouse" by his team-mates made an immediate impression on Bill Shankly, who decided to throw him straight in at the deep end.

Three goals in his first five league games followed and he went on to become a fixture in Shankly's Liverpool team.

Always last off the training pitch, Keegan transformed himself into one of England's finest forwards through sheer hard work and professionalism.

He hit 100 goals in 323 matches and his partnership with John Toshack is one of the finest in Liverpool's history.

RON YEATS

AS soon as Bill Shankly saw Ron Yeats he knew he had spotted a massive talent.

The fact Yeats went on to become the longest serving captain in Liverpool history and one of the finest defenders of his generation went some way to proving him right.

Yeats was famously introduced to the media when Shankly invited them to take a walk around the giant defender who went on to form the focal point of his defence.

It was a tough billing to live up to but one Yeats achieved with aplomb, clocking up 454 matches in a Liverpool shirt as he inspired the Reds to success as Shanks' first lieutenant on the pitch.

A £22,000 signing from Dundee United in 1961 he had the honour of being the first Liverpool skipper to raise the FA Cup aloft in 1965.